Content

1 **PREFACE** 3
2 **INTRODUCTION** 5
3 **GLOSSARY** 6
4 **HOW THE MARKET WORKS?** 9
    4.1 Market Drivers 10
    4.2 Price Never Moves in a Straight Line 14
    4.3 Reversion to Mean 21
        4.3.1 Key Points 23
5 **PULLBACKS** 25
    5.1 What's a Pullback? 25
        5.1.1 Single and Multi bar Pullbacks 26
    5.2 The More Pullbacks You Know, The More Prepared You Can Be 29
        5.2.1 Simple Pullbacks 29
        5.2.2 Complex Pullbacks 34
    5.3 Finding Pullbacks 46
    5.4 Measuring Pullbacks 51
        5.4.1 A Brief Introduction to Fibonacci (Fib) 51
        5.4.2 Fibonacci Retracements (Fib Ret) 52
    5.5 Key Points 56
6 **WHEN PULLBACK FAILS** 57
    6.1 How Pullback Fails? 57
    6.2 When Pullback Fails 60
    6.3 When Failed Pullback Fails 62
    6.4 Final Test of the Extremes 64
    6.5 Key Points 70
7 **HOW TO USE A PULLBACK?** 71
    7.1 Clues for Success 71
        7.1.1 Depth of a pullback 71
        7.1.2 Trend Bars 78
        7.1.3 Horizontal Support & Resistance Levels 81
        7.1.4 Knowing the Market Players and Timeframe 83
    7.2 Key Points 86
8 **THE BEST PULLBACK** 87
    8.1 Next Best Entry 87
    8.2 First Pullback in New Direction 90
    8.3 Combining Clues for First Pullbacks 92

		8.3.1	*Conviction of a Failed Pullback* *93*
		8.3.2	*Spotting Big Players at Market Extremes* *94*
	8.4		OTHER FORMS OF FIRST PULLBACKS 98
		8.4.1	*Reversal Patterns* *98*
	8.5		KEY POINTS 103
9	**BUILDING A CASE** **104**		
	9.1		STACKING PROBABILITIES 104
	9.2		KEY POINTS 110
10	**MASTERY – WHAT'S THAT ALL ABOUT?** **111**		
	10.1		FOUR STEPS TO MASTERY 112
	10.2		TECHNICAL MASTERY – THE JOURNEY 115
	10.3		MIND MASTERY – TRADING IN THE ZONE 116
11	**FURTHER DEVELOPMENT** **117**		

www.MarketApprentice.com

1 Preface

When I started trading the market, my first trading system was called the *Sniper*. The system relies on price action setups on the 5 minute chart in a trending market. The primary indicator is the 50 Exponential Moving Average (eMA) but you rely on a strong correlation amongst multiple timeframes. In short, if done correctly, this is a scalping technique which can generate profitable returns using low risk entries.

The system, till today, is one of the best systems that I learned. Apart from the intensity, the learning curve was steep and rewarding – especially in the area of timeframe correlations, price action and chart indicators. More importantly, while it was the first system that I traded (on a live account), it was also the first system that introduced me to trading market Pullbacks.

Of course, that was the first of many systems that I traded. Other systems that I picked up later provided insights into different market conditions – including any reversal and ranging markets. After a while, like many amateur traders, I realised that a system is just a set of rules governing your entries and exits. Through experience, I found out that, beyond any trading systems, there was a mysterious market theory called Price Action. (Yes, that included the market Pullback that was part of the market theory).

My curiosity pushed me to learn more and, along the way, I started to remove chart indicators and began to put my attention on price and price patterns only. At one point in my trading career, I was only trading using naked charts and price patterns. Since then, reading price action became the core of my trading and it helped me mature as a trader.

One day, during my trade review, I accidentally found a common theme amongst all the trades that I've made, I realised that I have been using pullbacks in all my trading systems. The more I explored that, the more I realised they exist in all markets and any market conditions. Some pullbacks were bigger than others, and some had a

www.MarketApprentice.com

higher probability of success. On top of that, I found out that Market Pullbacks can potentially provide low risk but high profitable entries.

With that, I hope to share my theory in this book. Hopefully, you can enjoy it sooner or later.

www.MarketApprentice.com

2 Introduction

"Sometimes the best things are just right in front of you."

Believe it or not, you see price pullbacks almost every time you open your price chart because it is inevitable that price is cycling and pulling back and forth all the time. However, many traders do not see it. That just goes to show that humans (including traders) can be so engrossed in their own thing that they often fail to see the obvious that is right in front of them.

While this book is primarily about pullbacks, this is also my way of breaking down information from what seems to be bulky blocks into little absorbable chunks and building them back into useful resources. By breaking the process down, you are able to spot the various clues in the market easily. The more clues you find, the more likely that you have a successful trade.

At the same time, never forget the bigger picture when trading. Since the big guns are the one with the deepest pocket, it makes sense to keep track of who those market leaders are. By keeping track, I don't mean searching for the traders' information. Instead, I am referring to understanding what and how price is reacting to certain challenges in the market. In fact, the more you understand price action, the easier you can spot the leader.

Trading price action pullbacks can be very profitable if done correctly. Hence, I hope to show you a variety of pullback patterns and hopefully you can use that as a starting point to fine tune your own trading. Learning to trade is a journey. However, once you built a solid foundation, the rest of the journey should be easier.

Also, it is profitable trading pullback if it is congruent with your trading beliefs. Hence, I hope to explain how, why and when trading pullbacks works. More importantly, you should also understand how, why and when they do not work.

3 Glossary

Glossary in alphabetical order

- Bear
    - An investor's term referring to the seller. Opposite of Bulls
- Big Players
    - Referring to large size market players including Central banks or major financial institutions. See also Mid Players and Small Players.
- Bull
    - An investor's term referring to the buyer. Opposite of Bears
- Ceiling
    - A term to represent a horizontal upper resistance line. Also known as horizontal resistance line. For a ceiling to be valid, the touches of two or more price highs are required.
- Channels
    - A price channel is a continuation price pattern that slopes upward or downward. Price is bounded by the Upper Resistance Line and Lower Support Line, creating a sloping (price) rectangle.
- Consolidated Market
    - A period of consolidation that is driven by the lack of volume, indecision or uncertainty. Irrespective of the reasons, the market lacks a clear leader in the market. Also known as a ranging market.
- DTD
    - Dominant Trend Direction.
    - This is the main direction in which the market is moving.
- Fib
    - Fibonacci
- Fib Ret
    - Fibonacci Retracement

- Floor
    - A term to represent a horizontal lower support lines. Also known as horizontal support line. For a floor to be valid, the touches of two or more price lows are required.
- H&S
    - Head & Shoulder. This is the name of a specific reversal pattern.
- Leg
    - A leg is the journey travelled by price in a single movement. For the purpose of this book, we assume that a simple pullback has 3 legs.
- Liquid Market
    - A market where there are plenty of buyers and sellers. With such volume of traders, the spread between the bid and ask prices tightens. Trade execution becomes easier and quicker as there is always an available buyer/seller. The opposite of a liquid market is a thin or illiquid market.
- Long
    - To take a position in the market with the view that price of the asset would go higher. Opposite of Short
- Lower Support Line
    - A line that is drawn using at least two price lows to form the lower support line. Opposite of Upper Resistance Line
- Market
    - Generally referring to the Financial Market.
- Mid Players
    - Referring to mid-size big market players including Mid-sized or small-sized banks, large hedge funds, market makers, large corporate or commercial companies. See also Big Players and Small Players.
- Naked charts
    - Clean charts using price bars only without any signals or indicators.

- Pin Bar
    - This can be a high test or a low test bar.
- Price Action (PA)
    - The movement of price within the financial market. PA also includes the areas of technical analysis and chart patterns. Some may even include candlestick analysis.
- Price Cyclicity
    - The nature of the market prices where is moves up and down – even when there is a clear trend.
- Pullbacks
    - Happens when price moves one bar (or more) against its previous bar that is moving in the direction of major trend.
- Short
    - To take a position in the market with the view that price of the asset would go lower. Opposite of Long
- Small Players
    - Referring to small size market players including Retail or private individual traders. See also Big Players and Mid Players.
- Upper Resistance Line
    - A line that is drawn using at least two price highs to form the upper resistance line. Opposite of Lower Support Line

4 How the Market Works?

The Financial Market is a common place where investors, buyers and sellers exchange their goods. Buyers look for sellers offering the lowest price and sellers look for buyers who are bidding for the highest price. In terms of market behaviour and price action, there isn't a huge difference between the financial market and, say, the property market or the food market.

Of course, the nature of the various financial markets is depending on the products bought or sold. This is true and is applicable for markets like the Currency market, Commodities market, Stock & Equities market, Futures market, Options market, Bond markets and more.

Each market is governed by its own rules and regulation - Some are centralised and some are decentralised. Due to these differences, some markets have more people than others, and that makes one market more liquid than the other.

With the boom of the internet and technology, buyers and sellers do not even need to meet up anymore. The truth is that, apart from price, buyers and sellers are not too bothered about with whom they are exchanging their goods. As long as the price is right, that's all that matters.

However, here is an important piece of advice that I learned a few years ago, as a market trader, it is wise to make yourself ***extremely familiar with one market*** before venturing into more. Since each market has its own personality, it takes time and extreme focus to understand it before you can master it. Once you do master it, you'll be making enough money that you won't be bothered to learn more.

4.1 Market Drivers

The financial market moves for different reasons and, more often than not, there's no or little point in finding out those reasons. Of course, I'll be lying if I said that the macro economy (as well as market sentiment) has no impact on the market, because they do. However, as a short to medium term trend trader, these fundamental reasons only give me a macro view of the overall trend but it does not give me trading opportunities.

But before explaining and describing what drives the market, the following are 4 (out of many) examples that are useful to get the ball rolling.

Gut Feeling

> John is an oil trader working in Goldman Sachs. He usually arrives at work before six in the morning but was running slightly late one day. John usually browses through his email on his way to work but, as he arrives in his London office that morning, he got a new email report from their research team titled "Bullish Outlook on Oil Price".
>
> Having some sizable positions on crude, John starts to go through the report and begins to rationalise his thoughts. While the report has been fairly reliable in the past, John was not comfortable with the report. He could not pinpoint what was wrong with it, but he decided to keep to his own bearish view instead. Already in profit, he decides to close his entire position before he goes on a break with his family.
>
> While John was having breakfast on his second day in the French Alps, he saw a news headline going "Violence in Iraq despite US pull out". As Iraq has the second largest proven oil reserves in the world, any unfavourable major events can easily disrupt the oil production and hence the prices of it.
>
> John carried on his breakfast with a smile.

Emotions

Kevin is a proprietary trader in a major Wall Street firm in New York city, and he has been a fairly successful one. His manager decided to push him a little further and agreed to let Kevin manage a much larger portfolio. Kevin was extremely excited about it. While the money was not significant to the bank, it was a large sum in Kevin's eyes.

One day (Day 1), Kevin took a long position in the interest rate futures. For every 0.01 move, he gains $27k. This position size was all new to him as he had never dealt with such a large position before. On Day 2, there was an unexpected announcement by the ECB President hinting a potential interest rate rise. As the news announcement went on, the market when manic on that information. However, because the news did not make sense, Kevin decides to hang in there.

Day 4, the volatility continues. At one stage, Kevin's position was at a loss of $500k and all that happened within 2 hours before it recovered slightly. Kevin started to question his own decision. At that point, the options included, (1) closing the position without risking further loss or (2) to increase his position to recover from his loss. Kevin's self confidence was at a minimal level, and there was much uncertainty in terms of how he should have dealt with the trade since Day 2.

Day 5, when Kevin walked into the office, deprived from sleep, Kevin was emotionally drained and decided that it did not look right anymore and made the decision to cut losses.

Day 6, the market finally resumed to normal. Unfortunately for Kevin, the rates recovered and moved in his favour.

www.MarketApprentice.com

Technical

Paul is a trader in a hedge fund. While he overlooks the operations – specifically the smooth entry and exits of trades – of the fund's trading desk, he is also a technical analysis expert.

Because Paul does not manage his own books (or portfolio), he only takes trades when Tim, the fund manager, sends him the trade instructions. As and when he receives those instructions, Paul has a specified time and price range where he must take those trades.

One day, the fund manager wanted him to take some positions in Google Inc. As soon as he got the instructions, Paul starts to analyse the technical settings of NASDAQ: GOOG. As Paul had five days to enter the trade, he started looking at the weekly chart before he moved down to the daily and 4 hour charts. Based on his analysis, he knew there were no trades on Day 1.

In fact, nothing happened until Day 4 when Paul finally got the signal that he wanted – a MACD crossover – showing the potential low of the week and the start of a trend continuation set up. As soon as the price hit a predefined support level, Paul bought those shares.

Fundamentals

Tom works in Rolls-Royce in the Treasury team within Group Finance. As the company has an international presence, half its transactions are dealt in foreign currencies – predominantly in US Dollar (USD). Meanwhile, because Rolls-Royce was a British company, most of their overhead costs are primarily dealt in pound sterling (GBP).

As the USD continues to drop against the GBP, Rolls-Royce's profit margin continues to be diluted. The only other way to protect the company from currency exchange rate risk was to hedge the currency positions.

As the trader within treasury, Tom reviews the macroeconomic indicators as well as company's currency position on a month to month basis before he presupposes how much hedging is required. Of course, this would also involve some mathematical calculation on expected sales figures as well as expected expenditure for the foreseeable future. While this may seem like a challenge for some companies, Rolls Royce's business model is pretty long term, and this is quite a mundane task for Tom.

Upon approval of the Finance Director, he typically takes a currency future position on behalf of Rolls Royce.

While John, Kevin, Paul and Tom might not be real people, the roles they played seem highly plausible. The ultimate goal of traders is to increase wealth and most professional traders enter the market for reasons that are unique to themselves. However, the market is driven by millions of individuals who represent either themselves or someone else (including big financial institutions) – just like John, Kevin, Paul and Tom.

My point is this, no one knows why the market moves the way they do because even some of the professional traders cannot explain themselves (Gut Feeling traders). Hence, if you, a retail trader, think that you know why the market is doing what it is doing, then you sound like you're in a dangerous position.

Also, while macro economic factors play an important role in the financial market, they probably play a less important role in an established trend and when looking at short to medium term markets. More importantly, many of the macro and fundamental information have been incorporated into price action. Believe it or not, fundamental investors are in the market too. However, the financial market is inefficient by nature and price would often reflect that information either before or after the data/news release.

4.2 Price Never Moves in a Straight Line

Now that you understand the drivers of the market (which is fairly unpredictable), you should also appreciate that the market prices never move in a straight line (for the same reasons). For your information, this is the honest truth about the market. In fact, the opposite is true – market prices **always** move up and down even when there is a clear trend. This phenomenon is known as **price cycle**.

Like it or not, this is true for all markets and all market conditions – including the trending, reversing or sideway market. The following are some examples to illustrate my point.

Trending Market

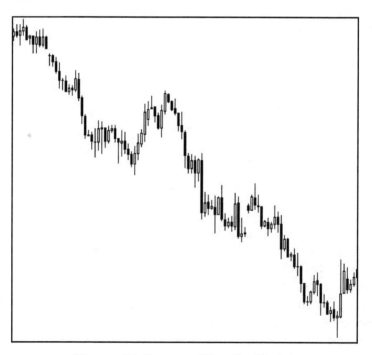

Diagram 4-1: Downward Trending Market

The above is a bear market and sellers were clearly the dominant players here. Although the sellers are taking control, it should be clear that the buyers and sellers constantly compete to take advantage of the market – no one ever gives in that easily without a good battle.

As you can see, each time price moves lower, buyers come into the market as price becomes cheaper. On the flipside, when price moves higher, sellers start to close their positions as they take profit. Of course, since there are more sellers than buyers, the sellers almost always take control of the market and continue to push the price lower.

The result of that was a zig-zagging market that is on its way down as the overall price moves lower and lower gradually.

Reversing Market

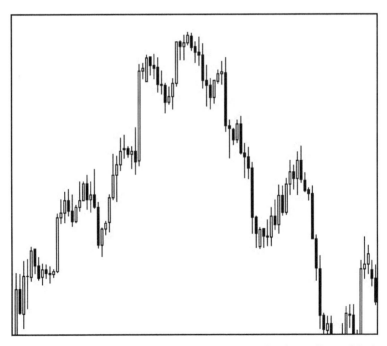

Diagram 4-2: Reversing Market – From an Up Market into a Down Market

www.MarketApprentice.com

Here the buyers were taking control of the market from the start and continuously push the price higher. Like the trending market, sellers were also looking for opportunities to sell even though buyers were in control.

Half way through the chart, buyers realised that they've done their best, and they can't seem to support the push anymore because price is now deemed "too expensive".

If the buyers have emptied their pockets and are incapable to supporting the uptrend, then sellers would be more than happy to enter the market at a "good" price. Hence, the sellers started selling the market and the buyers started closing their positions at the same time.

Again, as the sellers gradually take control, some buyers feel that there might be chances of recovery and they were hoping to remain in control. Thus, they try to build some small bullish positions along the downward market. In layman term, these buyers are called "*laggers*" – in case you might be laughing in disbelief, trust me, laggers exists in any marketplace.

As price continues to fall, some of the earlier buyers might decide to take profit and switch over to become a seller to take advantage of both the markets. On the other hand, some buyers who panic because prices are falling sharply might close their positions very quickly, and this would fuel the fall.

As you can see, the activities in the market place are endless and, thus, there are always reasons to cause prices to move up and down constantly.

Consolidating or Raging Market

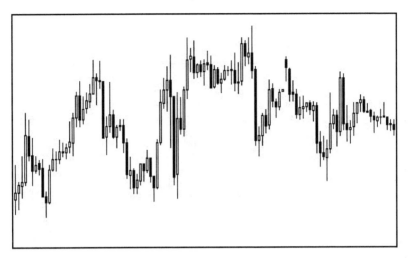

Diagram 4-3: Sideway Ranging Market

Even if price were to move side ways, it moves by cycling in a narrow price range. In this example, buyers and sellers are in equilibrium. However, don't expect price to move in a straight line even if they are in equilibrium. Instead, we only know that there isn't much tradable volume in the market since each time price reaches a *floor* (i.e. bottom of the price range), buyers would see that as an opportunity to buy. An alternative view is that there were not enough sellers to push price any lower.

The opposite is also true, and that happens when price reaches a *ceiling* (i.e. top of the price range). Sellers see that as an opportunity as well and would jump into the market to sell because price is now high enough. As there were insufficient buyers, price naturally moves lower when sellers come in.

As the market lacks volume, the floor and ceiling can often fluctuate a little since there is no single player that is taking control. Nonetheless, like any other market, nothing is ever permanent.

It is common to find traders or investors who would take advantage of these limitations and leverage it to make some short term profits.

Thus, different types of buyers and sellers will push the prices as a yo-yo.

Mixed Market

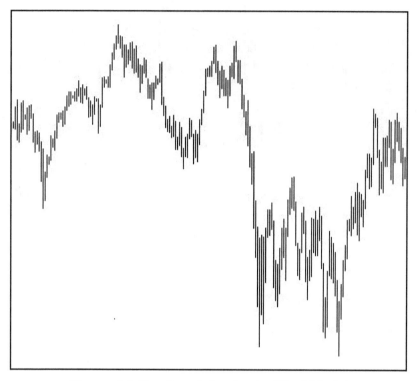

Diagram 4-4: Dow Jones Index showing Mixed Market

Secrets of Trading the First Pullback

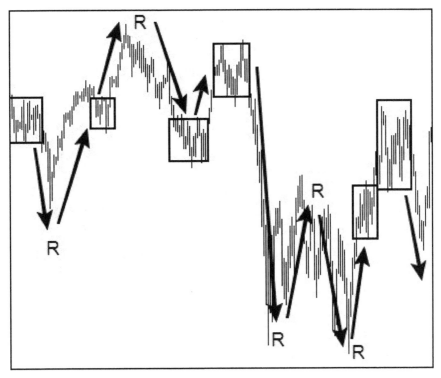

Diagram 4-5: Identifying Markets within Markets

Now that you've seen the different types of market conditions, it might be worth having a look at a mixed market. The Dow Jones Index (daily chart) in Diagram 4-4 is another example of how the market never moves in a straight line. On top of that, price moves from one market (condition) to another.

If it's not obvious to you, then have a look at Diagram 4-5 where you can see there are trending (arrows), reversing (R) and ranging (rectangle box) markets in there and all of them acting in random sequences. While price is cycling within the three markets, the above is also a good example of how price is cycling actively even in the bigger picture (or macro market).

www.MarketApprentice.com

Timeframes and Liquidity

Price cycles in all timeframes. In other words, you can find price cycling within the Trending, Reversing and Ranging markets and that can happen in the daily, 4 hourly, 60 minutes, 15 minutes, 5 minutes and even the 1 minute timeframe.

However, for price to do that, the market needs to be liquid. A good indication of a liquid market is when you find it relatively easy to execute your trade and you can do so at or close to your desired price. This is possible because, when in a liquid market as the currency market or even some Fortune 500 companies, you can find buyers and sellers of all sizes exchanging financial assets all the time.

Just to be clear, price continues to cycle even in an illiquid market. However, it is easier to find price cycles in smaller timeframes when the market is liquid.

4.3 Reversion to Mean

Not only does the market move in cycles, it actually moves in a certain pattern and that pattern is driven by the concept of **Mean Reversion**. That means, the market almost always return to the mean or average price after it moves away from it.

For simplicity, it might be easier if you think of it as a pendulum. Imagine a pendulum swinging from left to right and back, the centre of the pendulum is like a mean position, and the pendulum would always get pulled back to the centre but then it also gets pushed away from the centre.

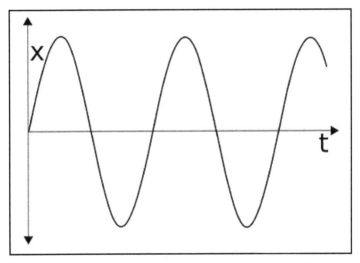

Diagram 4-6: Reversion to Mean – Distance from Mean (x) Vs Time (t) Graph

The diagram above shows the distance (x) of the pendulum away from the mean position (zero) against time (t). As you can see, price always moves away from the mean before it reaches an *extreme*. Price then reverts to the mean from the extreme as if there is a **magnetic field** pulling it back to the centre.

Price action works in the same way when travelling in cycles. While the mean of a pendulum is constantly zero, the mean of the market price is *constantly moving*. In fact, in a trending market, price doesn't even return to the mean before it moves back into the trend direction.

Another interesting fact that you must be aware is that it is ***difficult to predict*** how far price moves away before it is pulled towards the mean again. Many have tried to pick the extremes (i.e. market tops and bottoms), and, unfortunately, that's not a wise decision. In fact, with-trend traders would wait for price action clues *after* price topped or bottomed before buying or selling in the new trend direction.

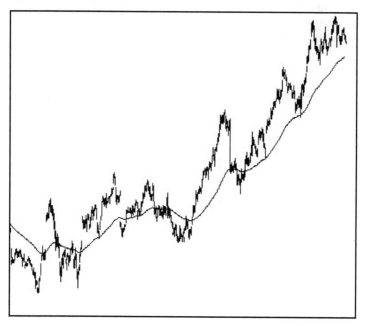

Diagram 4-7: Google Inc showing Reversion to Mean

As shown above, the Google Inc (daily) chart shows that price has been cycling up and down constantly. As part of price cycle, it is also constantly being pulled back towards the mean price (moving average line) before moving away from it again.

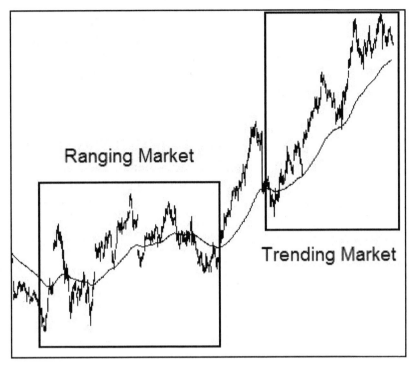

Diagram 4-8: Range Market Vs Trending Market

Let's make this slightly more interesting, if you split the chart in 2, you can find a ranging market and a trending market in there. In the ranging market, price is crossing from one side of the mean price to the other and that is somewhat similar to the pendulum.

On the other hand, in a trending market, price usually stays on one side of the mean price only - this is a good indication of a strong trend. Nonetheless, price continues to cycle and it is still being drawn back to the mean price once in a while before moving higher again.

4.3.1 Key Points

Here are the summaries and key pointers for this section:

- Markets are driven by multiple reasons that are difficult to quantify and that's including human emotions, fundamentals, technical analysis or any other unknown reasons.
- Price never moves in a straight line. In fact, it is constantly cycling up and down.
- While price cycles are random as they switch between trending, reversing and consolidating in an unpredictable sequence. Nonetheless, you can still find some predictable patterns within those random movements.
- Market extremes are where those "magnetic fields" are strongest, and you can expect a pull towards the mean (or average) price from those extremes – also known as Reversion to the Mean. However, never try to pick tops or bottoms.

5 Pullbacks

5.1 What's a Pullback?

Market or price action **Pullback**, by definition, happens when price moves at least one bar against the dominant trend direction (DTD). A pullback is a price movement that moves in the opposite direction of the trend but it is only temporarily price movement before it resumes back into the main market direction.

Pullbacks are sometimes referred to as price *Retracements* or *Corrections*. Some may even just call it a *Dip*. It doesn't matter what you call it as long as the temporary countertrend movement resumes in the main market direction later and it does so by breaking beyond the recent price extreme. If price does not go beyond the recent extreme, then the pullback could reverse, or it could consolidate.

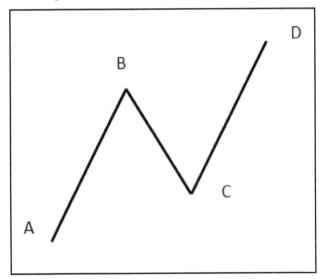

Diagram 5-1: ABCD Pattern

For the purpose of illustration, we will use be using the ABCD pattern to explain the details of simple pullbacks because the ABCD pattern is a perfect example of it.

Secrets of Trading the First Pullback

On top of that, a simple pullback always moves in three legs. Using the diagram above, in an uptrend, AB is the first leg where price is moving towards the DTD. This is followed by the second leg (BC) and the cycle is completed as soon as the final leg (CD) moves beyond B.

Just to be clear, the activity a pullback is only represented by BC. However, for the sake of completeness, a pullback (BC) must **remain between A and B** and **it must include CD** where D moves beyond B. If not, that would be considered a failed pullback – further discussion on failed pullback can be found in Section 6.1.

Note:

A leg is the journey travelled by price in a single movement. For the purpose of this book, we can assume that a simple pullback has 3 legs. You may find that other traders refer them differently.

5.1.1 Single and Multi bar Pullbacks

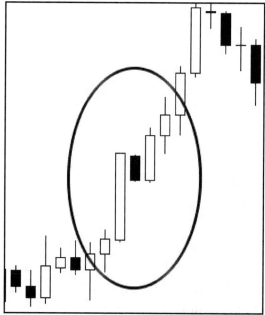

Diagram 5-2: Example of Single Bar Pullback

Secrets of Trading the First Pullback

The diagram above shows a ***single bar*** pullback example. It shows how a pullback can be short and quick. Since the definition states that price needs to move at least one bar against the DTD. In this example, the trend bar (prior to the single seller bar in the circle) represents AB and the seller bar is BC. The next trend bar that moved above the entire seller bar is CD. Hence, this is a valid pullback even though the ABCD pattern is not obvious.

In this example, the entire ABCD pullback can also be considered as a single leg since the 3 legs are really small.

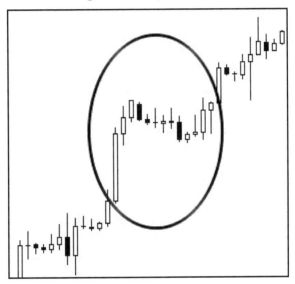

Diagram 5-3: Example of Multi Bar Pullback

The next diagram (above) is a ***multi bar*** pullback, and it shows a few seller bars before price resumed back into the DTD.

A pullback can be shallow or deep, and it can be fast or slow. While the depth and speed of the pullback are independent of each other, they are often influenced by the market drivers at that point in time, and no one really knows when any of them happens. Again, we will dive into the characteristics of pullbacks in a later section. For now, just appreciate that pullbacks can happen in various shapes, depths and speeds.

www.MarketApprentice.com

Also, do appreciate the fact that pullbacks are natural occurrences in the financial market, and these are trading opportunities for traders. However, unless a trader understands how pullbacks work, a pullback is nothing more than another price pattern.

5.2 The More Pullbacks You Know, The More Prepared You Can Be

In case you have not realised, in order for price to cycle, there **must** be a pullback. Think about it, price needs to pull back before it can push forward. And the repetition of pulling back and pushing forward is what contributes to a price cycle.

As mentioned in Section 4.2, where the market is liquid, price will cycle in all market conditions, in any timeframe and any direction. If that is true, then this must also mean that *prices will make pullbacks in any market conditions, any timeframe* and *any direction* as well.

As traders, instead of trying to predict the future, it is more useful to recognise these pullbacks and then perform your analysis based on how these pullbacks behave. Remember that trading is about stacking up the probabilities in our favour, and this is exactly what you are trying to achieve here. By recognising the various types of pullbacks, you can pick trades that have a higher probability of success in order. Once we have the probabilities in our favour, we take the trade.

For the purpose of illustration, I have grouped market pullbacks in two distinct groups – simple and complex pullbacks.

5.2.1 Simple Pullbacks

A simple pullback should be in the shape of an ABCD pattern. Hence, they are usually fairly obvious and easy to spot while complex pullbacks might take a little longer to form.

However, a simple pullback can remain simple, or it can evolve to become a complex pullback as well. Since we don't know when that happens, it is important to *manage your risk and money wisely*.

If you find yourself spending too much time looking for simple pullbacks, it's probably because they are either complex ones, or they are not a pullback at all. Either way, when that happens, you should just ignore it and look for trading opportunities elsewhere.

The following are more examples of simple pullbacks.

Secrets of Trading the First Pullback

Deep Pullback

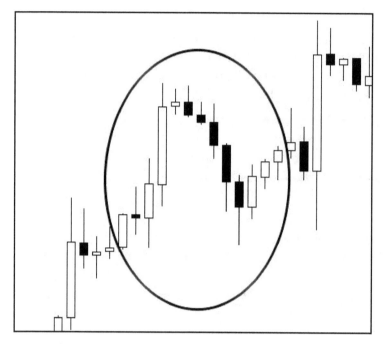

Diagram 5-4: Deep Pullback

Let's start by having a look at a deep pullback. This is probably amongst the easier price pattern to spot. Characteristics of a deep pullback are:

- In a deep pullback, the price moves a significant distance against the DTD, and this is the key identifier of a deep pullback.
- It can be happen quickly, or it can happen slowly. In other words, it can also be a sharp pullback even if it is a deep one.
- It is usually made up of a few consecutive seller (or buyer) bars with one or two bars that are relatively longer than the rest. However, the key is the distance travelled (as opposed to the type of bar).
- Reading price action in the diagram above, in a deep pullback, the bears are usually trying to show their dominants. However, not realising that the bulls are still strong, the bulls

usually come back into the market just before the bears managed to build confidence.

Shallow Pullback

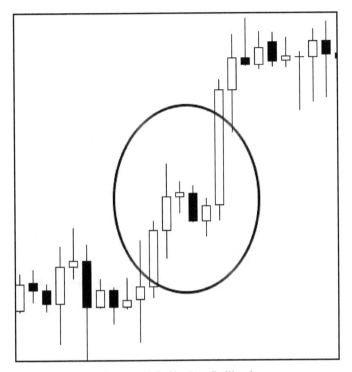

Diagram 5-5: Shallow Pullback

Characteristics of a shallow pullback:

- The pullback moves very little against the DTD. This is the key identifier of a shallow pullback.
- It can be happen quickly, or it can happen slowly. It can also be a flat pullback if turns out to be sideway movement.
- It usually comprises a mixture of doji and small bodied bars. Sometimes, you can also expect to see long tailed bars. The type of bars you get is less important as it's the movement of the bars that matters.

Secrets of Trading the First Pullback

- A shallow pullback is usually an indication that the market is one-sided. Reading the price action in the diagram above, the bears only managed to push price slightly in there favour, and the bulls were already back in the market. Hence, price is expected to move relatively far after the pullback.

Sharp Pullback

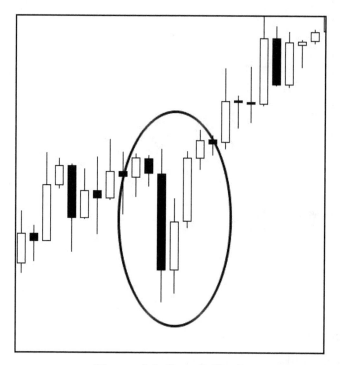

Diagram 5-6: Sharp Pullback

Characteristics of a sharp pullback:

- This is usually a very quick pullback and the speed of the pullback is the key identifier.
- Although a sharp pullback is typically made up of only one or two bars, it can also happen when you have multiple bars, but there is a clear counter trend movement within a relatively short span of time.

- The sharp pullback can be considered a deep pullback. Having said that, you can occasionally find sharp pullback that is relative shallow. Either way, the idea is to keep a close watch and not to predict the market.
- The price action above showed some selling strength initially. With such a strong bear trend bar, the sellers were hoping to attract more sellers into the market but only realised that the buyers were still in control and that push did not go far.

Flat Pullback

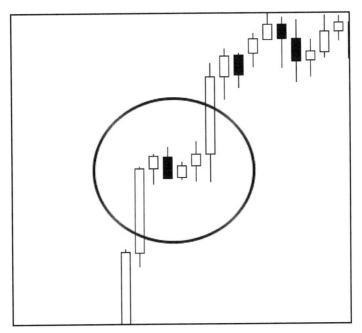

Diagram 5-7: Flat Pullback

Characteristics of a flat pullback:
- A flat pullback is considered a shallow pullback. However, it is slightly more extreme than your typical shallow pullback because the market only moves sideways, with very little countertrend movement, before it resumes in the DTD.
- The sideways movement is key identifier for this pullback.

- A flat pullback is an indication of a very strong market.
- Based on the price action above buyers often fail to find a good long entry into the DTD because price barely retraces. Many waited for a minor reversal to show confirmation that price is correcting itself – unfortunately, due to the big players driving the market, price continues its bull run before traders even realise it.

5.2.2 Complex Pullbacks

The purpose of this section is to give you the tools to navigate in the market and, more importantly, to stay out of it when in a complex pullback. In other words, when you see a complex pullback, I would strongly suggest that you should stay out of the market. Complex pullbacks happen when price steps into a consolidating phase. It then remains consolidated for awhile before it resumes into the DTD. No one really knows how long it remains consolidated before it moves again.

On top of that, if you struggle to recognise the price patterns on your charts, I believe it is only reasonable to say that you should stay away from it and find another clearer chart where the probability of making a profit is higher. Trading is about take trades where you feel right, the setup should be recognisable within seconds and nothing more.

Note:

Before we start looking at examples of complex pullbacks, it is crucial to remember that simple pullbacks are price patterns that are much more profitable trades because you either see them or you don't.

Don't be fooled by the idea that you should make money in every market. In fact, many professional traders only trade on simple pullbacks because that's all they need.

Rising / Falling Wedge Pullback

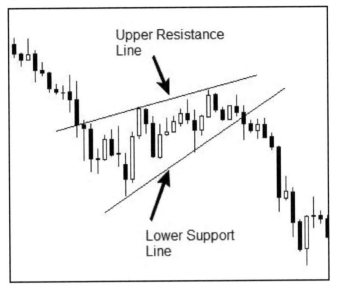

Diagram 5-8: Rising Wedge

Secrets of Trading the First Pullback

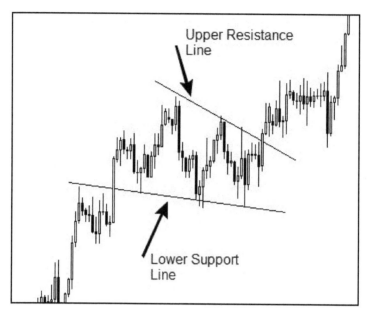

Diagram 5-9: Falling Wedge

Characteristics of a rising / falling wedge:

- A rising wedge occurs when you have a price action pullback that is sloping upwards when in a downward trending market (as shown in Diagram 5-8). Meanwhile, the price range of the pullback becomes narrower as it goes against the DTD.
- When price makes a pullback, you can eventually spot an upper resistance line on the top and a lower support line at the bottom, sitting between prices – as shown in both diagrams above. Both the lines converge as price action becomes narrower.
- As the wedge starts to narrow, that is an indication that the market is becoming more indecisive. As investors see this, they would also begin to sit out of the market. In other words, this becomes a self-fulfilling prophecy as the wedge continues to narrow even more.
- Like a spring being compressed, price gets squeezed to the point where it has no choice but to burst out with momentum.

Secrets of Trading the First Pullback

- In a rising wedge, the pullback ends when price breaks below the lower support line and vice versa for a falling wedge.
- All the above applies to a falling wedge but in the opposite direction.

Note:

See the Glossary page for definition of Upper Resistance Line *and* Lower Support Line.

Rising / Falling Flag Pullback

Diagram 5-10: Rising Flag

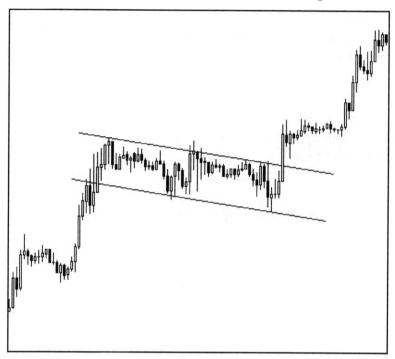

Diagram 5-11: Falling Flag

Characteristics of a rising / falling flag:

- A rising/falling flag is very similar to a rising/falling wedge with the exception that the price range stays consistent as price moves against the DTD. In other words, the upper resistance line and lower support line are parallel to each other as price pullbacks. Thus, creating a small price channel.
- Just like the rising/falling wedge, the pullback ends as soon as price breaks out of the channel towards the DTD.
- However, since price does not converge, it does not break out like a spring either. Thus, it can be challenging when identifying where price turns.
- Occasionally, price would continue in the new direction (against the DTD) regardless and, hence, making it a reversal pattern instead of a pullback.

Sideway / Rectangles Pullback

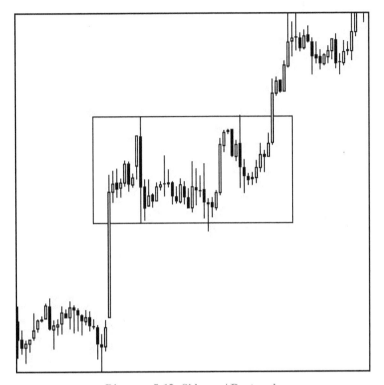

Diagram 5-12: Sideway/ Rectangle

Characteristics of a sideway / rectangle pullback:

- A sideway / rectangle pullback is a sideway price movement, and it can be defined using a rectangle box where the top and bottom limit of the box is drawn using the horizontal upper resistance line (for the top) and horizontal bottom support line (for the bottom).
- Remember that it is important to have at least *two price touches* on both the top and bottom respectively to define the boundary of the rectangle. Without that confirmation, the pullback could even end up as a wedge or a flag pullback instead.

Secrets of Trading the First Pullback

- To a certain extend, a sideway pullback is essentially a flat pullback but comprises of more price action and movements.

Double Bottom / Top Pullback

Diagram 5-13: Double Bottom Pullback

Characteristics of a double bottom / top pullback:

- A double bottom pullback occurs when price retraces to the same price level twice before it resumes back into the DTD. In an uptrend, this happens when price retraces to touch the horizontal bottom support line twice before resuming to its main trend direction.
- While double bottom is a typical reversal pattern, it is not uncommon in trend continuation pullbacks. In fact,

Secrets of Trading the First Pullback

sometimes, rectangle pullbacks are deemed a double bottom pullback as well.
- Looking at the diagram above, the sellers attempted to sell the market but the buyers took control, forming a shallow pullback (left circle). After that, the sellers made their second attempt to push the price lower. While they looked successful initially, the buyers stepped in again at the price near the first attempt. This time round, the buyers were serious, and, from then on, they took charge of the market.
- All the above applies to a double top pullback as well but in the opposite direction.

Ascending / Descending Triangles Pullback

Diagram 5-14: Ascending Triangle

Secrets of Trading the First Pullback

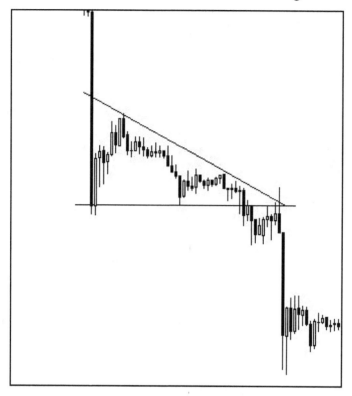

Diagram 5-15: Descending Triangle

Characteristics of an ascending /descending triangle pullback:

- In Diagram 5-14, an ascending triangle pullback was formed when there was a relatively strong horizontal upper resistance line that was holding price from going higher. Each time price hits the line, it drops. However, each time it drops, the fall weakens. Thus, it starts making higher lows and, like a wedge, price started to converge.
- From a market psychology point of view, this seems to suggest that there was a large sell order placed at a fix price (where horizontal upper support line is located). Each time the buyers push price to that level, price drops as part of the order got triggered. This continues for awhile until the entire

www.MarketApprentice.com

Secrets of Trading the First Pullback

order was cleared and once there weren't any more sellers, price pushed higher.
- The opposite is true for a descending triangle.
- Ascending /descending triangles are one of the more attractive patterns to trade. Since price only moves towards the dominant trend direction, the extremes are not retested. However, the problem (like all other complex pullbacks) is that you don't know what to expect until it happens.
- Sometimes, you may find price breaking out of the triangle where it goes against the DTD too. Thus, this becomes a reversal pattern instead of a pullback.

Pennants Pullback

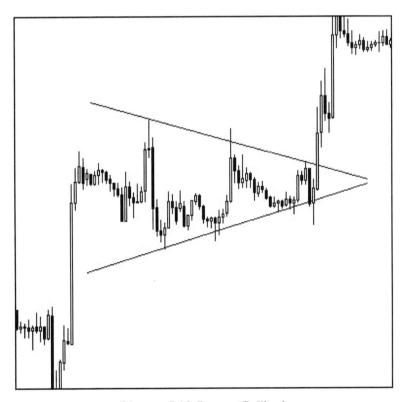

Diagram 5-16: Pennant Pullback

Characteristics of a pennant pullback:

- Pennant is similar to a symmetrical triangle. It has a sloping upper resistance line, a sloping lower support line and both these lines converge to form a triangle (as shown above).
- Just like the wedge, buyers and sellers are consolidating, and the consolidation causes price to funnel towards an equilibrium point. Typically, price would start moving again before it reaches the extreme tip of the triangle.
- Pennants are nice to look at in hindsight. However, it is challenging to pinpoint when price would resume back into the DTD again.
- Like the other triangles, it is not surprising if this turns out to be a reversal pattern.

Widening Wedge Pullback

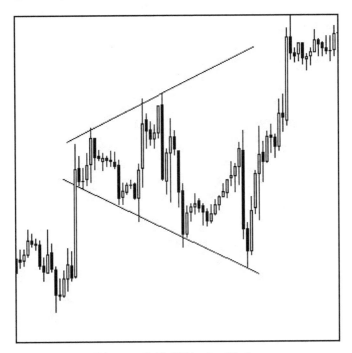

Diagram 5-17: Widening Wedge

Characteristics of a widening wedge pullback:

- A widening wedge happens when the upper resistance line and the lower support line diverge. While price looks like it's potentially forming a simple pullback, price would start to swing vigorously on both ends.
- The buyers and sellers are definitely in a war. Unlike previous converging pullbacks, where buyers and sellers sat aside to wait for further confirmation, this is a tug-of-war in the making. Buyers would push price higher but stronger sellers would take over as soon as it reaches a higher price. The buyers came in again as soon as price moves lower and the buyers pushed price even higher in the next round. The process repeats itself until a clear winner emerged.

Secrets of Trading the First Pullback

- As you can imagine, a widening wedge is one of the more complex pullbacks and it is where most new traders often get trapped.

5.3 Finding Pullbacks

Now that you understand the idea of market pullbacks and you have a rough idea of what they look like, let's move another step forward and try to figure out how you can find the pullbacks.

Remember that price never goes in a straight line? I'm sure you do. With that, pullbacks are easier to spot if you think of price action as price that is cycling up and down. Another important key concept that you need to know about price is that, for price to cycle higher, you need a *swing low* before it moves to create a *swing high* (and vice versa).

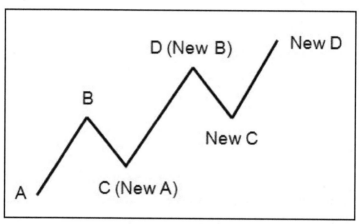

Diagram 5-18: Repeated ABCD

Looking at the diagram above, you can see how the ABCD pattern is cycling up and down repeatedly in an uptrend. Starting from point A and B on the left, watch how each price action pullback creates a swing low (C) which is followed by a swing high (D).

In order to spot a new pullback, change the C and D to a New A and New B. As cycle repeats itself, another pullback develops to create a

Secrets of Trading the First Pullback

new swing low (New B) and a ***new swing high*** (New D). As you can imagine, this carries on for awhile as long as price continues to cycle in the DTD.

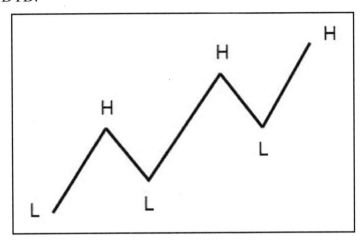

Diagram 5-19: Defining Swing Highs and Lows

Instead of counting the A, B, C and Ds, a common way of looking for pullbacks is to use the annotation of swing highs (H) and swing lows (L). Hence, it is useful if you think of price pullbacks as they cycle with alternating highs and lows.

Secrets of Trading the First Pullback

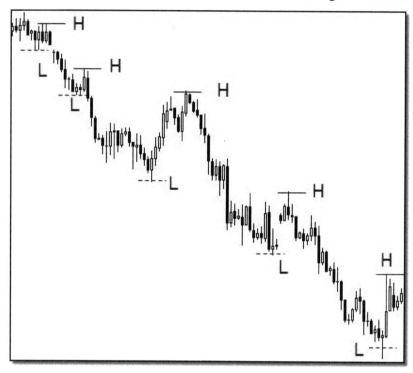

Diagram 5-20: Highs and Lows in Downward Trending Market

Secrets of Trading the First Pullback

Diagram 5-21: Highs and Lows in Reversal Market

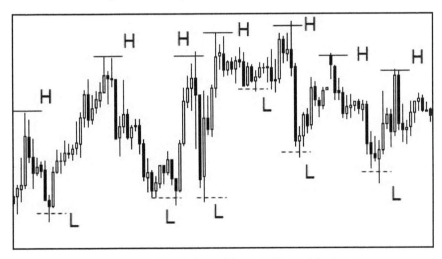

Diagram 5-22: Highs and Lows in Range Market

As shown in the three diagrams above, the short lines represent the highs (H) and lows (L) of each price cycle. In a downtrend, a H-L-H-L would represent one cycle, and H is where the pullback is located. Meanwhile, in an uptrend, a L-H-L-H would represent another cycle, and L is where the pullback is located.

Evidently, there is a pullback in each price cycle and price cycles happen in any market conditions. Hence, if you struggle to find price action pullbacks, all you need to do is draw the highs and lows on your charts and you can almost see them immediately.

In case you haven't noticed, pullbacks and swings are linked and they are pretty much interchangeable. Reading price action using swing highs and lows is a ***great way for spotting pullbacks*** and pullbacks are good with-trend market entries. This is also a good alternative to ABCD patterns. Both Swing H and L are equally good when compared to ABCD patterns. More importantly, neither is better than another as both are equally good. In fact, the best ones are the ones that what works for you. So make sure to try both and find out for yourself.

5.4 Measuring Pullbacks

The Fibonacci Retracement (Fib Ret) is a powerful tool to use when identifying key areas where pullbacks end before moving back into the DTD. However, since price action is driven by market players, they are not exact science and they have their limitations too. Hence, do not worship the tool but use it in moderation. More importantly, use it along other tools that you may already have.

5.4.1 A Brief Introduction to Fibonacci (Fib)

Fibonacci numbers were introduced by Leonardo Pisano Bogollo (1170-1250), an Italian mathematician from Pisa. He is known to have discovered the numbers, which are a sequence of numbers where each successive number is the sum of the two previous numbers.

Example: 1, 1, 2, 3, 5, 8, 13, 21, 34, 55, 89, 144, 233, 377, 610......

As shown, when you sum a number (n) to its preceding number ($n-1$), you'll get the next in sequence ($n+1$).

For example, when you add 1+1, you get 2? When you add 5+8, you get 13? Or when you add 233+377, you get 610? And so on. The sequence extends to infinity and contains many unique mathematical properties.

These numbers are based on Liber Abaci – a book on arithmetic by Leonardo of Pisa, known later by his nickname Fibonacci. Liber Abaci was among the first Western books to describe Hindu–Arabic numbers traditionally described as "Arabic Numerals"

The main ratio used is 0.618 – this is found by dividing one Fibonacci number into the next in sequence Fibonacci number (Example: Both 55/89 or 377/610 = 0.618). Meanwhile, the inverse of that is commonly known as the Golden Ratio – 1.618. Other ratios include 0.236, 0.382 and 0.764.

It is understood that Fibonacci numbers and its ratios represent many natural phenomena. Of course, that happens to include the financial market – since prices are driven by human beings (as humans too are part natural phenomena).

5.4.2   Fibonacci Retracements (Fib Ret)

As these Fibonacci (Fib) numbers can be applied in technical analysis, Fib ratios have been used by many traders to identify areas where price would potentially reverse (at the end of the retracements or pullbacks) back into the DTD.

Without any surprises, the typical Fib ratios that are used include 23.6%, 38.2%, 50%, 61.8%, 76.4% and 100%. However, 38.2%, 50% and 61.8% are known as the key ratios and have been found to be more useful than the rest. Hence, many technical traders also associate this as a Fib Ret ratio.

The 50% Fib Ret is not a Fibonacci number. Nonetheless, this number is derived from Dow Theory's assumption that price generally retraces to half its primary price movement.

Fib Ret ratios are more useful when price is in a trending market because it is assumed that price is likely to continue in its major trend direction.

With that, let's have a look at some examples.

38.2% Fib Pullback

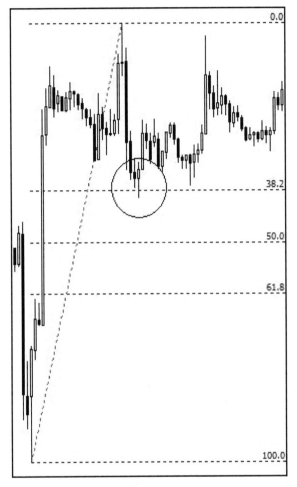

Diagram 5-23: 38.2% Fib Pullback

As shown above, when you draw the Fib Ret ratios, the 38.2% ratio showed that it was a good area for price to reverse back into the DTD.

Since 38.2% was relatively shallow (compared to 50% or 61.8%), it can be assumed to be a shallow pullback. Hence, it carries the characteristics of a shallow pullback which was discussed earlier.

50% Fib Pullback

Diagram 5-24: 50% Fib Pullback

The next example is the 50% Fib Ret. This level is the mid point (between A and B) and it is quite common for prices to bounce in the area between the 50% and 61.8% levels.

The sharp pullback above shows that price had respected the 50% ratio before it started heading north again.

www.MarketApprentice.com

61.8% Fib Pullback

Diagram 5-25: 61.8% Fib Pullback

61.8% Fib is a pullback that has passed the mid point. While the terminology is less important, as a Fibonacci user, we need to remember the 50%-61.8% is a favoured retracement area in the financial market (as mentioned previously).

Looking at the diagram above, price came down and tested the 50% Fib before it moved further down to test the 61.8% Fib level. As you can imagine, it is not uncommon for price to test each ratio before settling for one.

www.MarketApprentice.com

5.5 Key Points

Here are the summaries and key pointers for this section:

- A Pullback, by definition, happens when price moves at least one bar against the dominant trend direction (DTD). It is only temporarily counter-trend price movement before it resumes back into the main market direction.
- The more types of pullback you learn, the more you are ready and prepared for the market.
- Simple pullbacks are easy to spot, and they are profitable set ups.
- Complex pullbacks are more difficult to spot but keep practicing, and you'll be able to see them coming in advance.
- Fibonacci Retracement ratio is a good tool to help identify areas of a potential reversal of price back into the DTD. 38.2%, 50% and 61.8% are known as key Fib Ret ratios.
- If you struggle to find pullbacks using ABCD patterns, a good alternative to spotting pullbacks is by spotting swing highs (H) and swing lows (L).

6 When Pullback Fails

"Know thy self, know thy enemy. A thousand battles, a thousand victories."

– Sun Tzu

As Sun Tzu says it, knowing yourself is only part of the games, if you know your enemy too, you can win many battles.

If you want to succeed in using price action pullbacks in your trading, you need to know how pullbacks fail too because, when it happens, you are prepared for it. Once you learn to navigate the market, through successful and failed pullbacks, you are certain to progress pretty far in this career.

With that, this section is to explore price action leading to a pullback failure and what our options are when it happens.

6.1 How Pullback Fails?

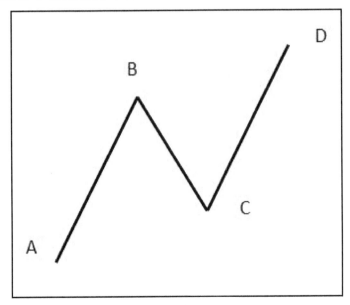

Diagram 6-1: Simple Pullback

Secrets of Trading the First Pullback

Using the example of a simple uptrend pullback, we define a pullback when price moves against the dominant trend direction (DTD) momentarily (from B to C) before it reverses back into the DTD (from C to D).

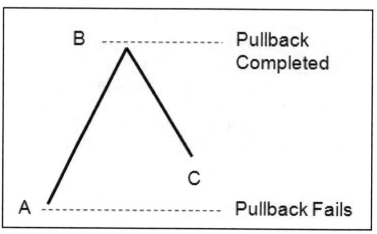

Diagram 6-2: When Pullbacks are Completed Vs When Pullback Fails

As mentioned earlier, the terminology of a pullback only represents BC. However, for the sake of completeness, a pullback must include CD where D clearly moves beyond B. On the other hand, if C clearly moves below A, BC is no longer a pullback and *that is the point where the pullback fails*.

Just a reminder, it is important that a break below point A shows *conviction*, because a convicted failure represents a market leader taking charge. To illustrate my point, let's look at an example.

Secrets of Trading the First Pullback

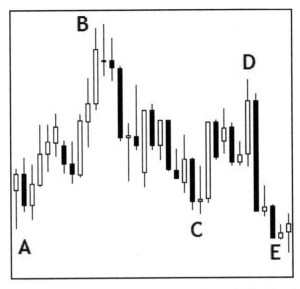

Diagram 6-3: Failed Pullback on USDCHF (Daily Chart)

The Swissy (USDCHF) currency pair daily chart above shows a failed pullback. Starting from the left of the chart, the move down to C (after AB made a new high) looked like a normal pullback. In fact, the small-bodied doji (bar C) seems like a reasonable indication to show that the sellers have had enough, and the bullish trend bar after that was a good signal showing that the buyers were back.

However, CD did not go beyond B. Instead, price turned at D to move south. The pullback became invalidated as soon as price moved below A, and bar E was where it happened. When that happens, E becomes the first lower low (LL) in the uptrend.

6.2 When Pullback Fails

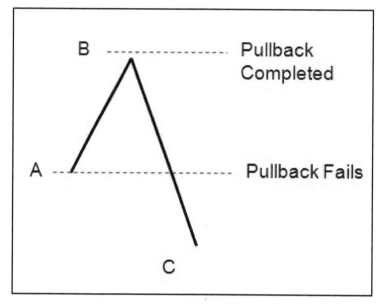

Diagram 6-4: When Pullbacks Fail

When C moves below A, that means the pullback has failed. This is an important price pattern for trend traders to remember because, when a pullback fails, *the chances are high that the market trend has ended.*

However, this does not imply that the market is going to start trending in the opposite direction immediately. Many new traders assume that when the trending market ends, you'll get a reversal market immediately. Unfortunately, that's not the case.

When a trend ends, there is a 50:50 chance that price would reverse into the new direction or it could start moving sideways. In fact, if you get a sideways market, you could still find the market trending again in the old direction at the end of the sideway market, and that is not surprising at all.

Secrets of Trading the First Pullback

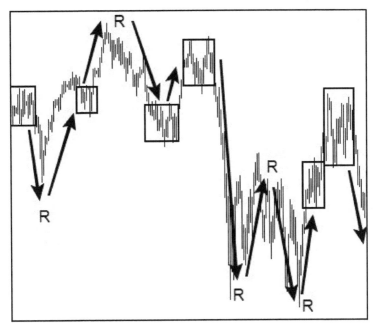

Diagram 6-5: Dow Jones Index showing Mixed Market

The Dow Jones Index above (taken from Diagram 4-5) showed how price moved from one market to another in no particular order. This just goes to show that the market doesn't necessarily reverses immediately after a trending market ends even though it could.

To sum it up, here are the potential outcomes when a pullback fails:

- Market moves sideways
    - After that, it continues in the original trend direction, or
    - After that, it reverses and starts a new trend in the opposite direction
- It reverses and starts a new trend in the opposite direction

As you can see, the market works in its mysterious ways. However, while the market is random, we can still narrow down the options and be prepared when either of them happens.

www.MarketApprentice.com

6.3 When Failed Pullback Fails

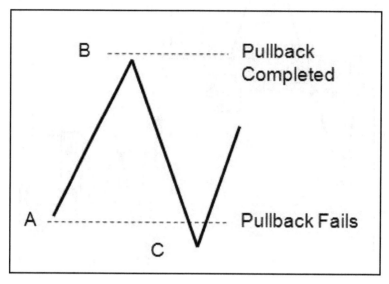

Diagram 6-6: Defining the Failure of a Failed Pullback

Let's push this one notch higher. Now that you're aware of the importance of point A and B in an ABCD simple pullback pattern, let's explore these two points slightly more.

As mentioned earlier, a failed pullback is a good indication of change of trend. However, it is not surprising that you can come across a failed pullback that fails. Essentially, in an uptrend, this happens when price moves below point A but fails to sustain the drop. In other words, you have a false break below Point A. This is not surprising as well since Point A is also a horizontal support level.

As you can see, that is why it is important to ***get a clear break*** below Point A before you can be certain that the market condition has changed. If there is no conviction to break below Point A, which was a good indication that there were insufficient sellers to push the price lower, buyers see that as an opportunity to buy the market at an even cheaper price.

The key at this stage is to start looking for clues in the market again. One of the approaches here is to figure out which market player is

Secrets of Trading the First Pullback

buying – is it a big player or a mid player? If you find a strong bullish pin bar followed by bullish trend bars, the chances are high that the big buyers are back. If not, then be prepared for even more uncertainty.

For smart traders, the real confirmation that the bulls are back is when you get a clear break above point B. This is also important because, without that confirmation, price can even make a second attempt to test Point A. When that happens, there is a possibility that neither the buyers nor sellers are dominant anymore. In fact, price could have shifted into a ranging market before you realised.

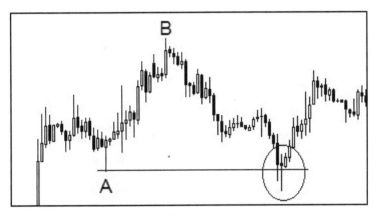

Diagram 6-7: Gold (1 hour chart) showing a Failure of a Failed Pullback

The Gold (1 Hour) chart above showed a failure of a failed pullback (circle). Price made a small spike below Point A but managed to close with a pin bar where the body of the bar was completely above Point A. All these price action are clues to show the probability of convicted break was fairly low.

In this example, price did not show much conviction after the failure of the failed pullback and price started to wonder sideways. Bars with long tails and small bodies are classic examples where there was little conviction from either side of the market. In other words, the failure of a failed pullback was the start of even more uncertainty.

Secrets of Trading the First Pullback

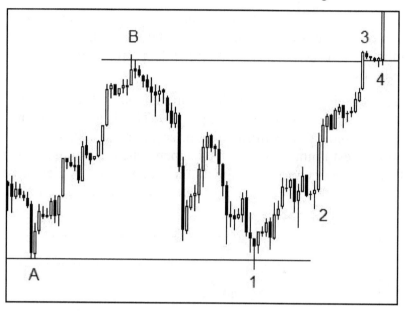

Diagram 6-8: SP500 Index (4 Hour chart) Shows a long Continuation after a Failure of Failed Pullback

The S&P 500 Index showed another failed pullback that failed on a 4 hour chart (bar 1). Looking at price action, this was somewhat similar to a double bottom pullback (bar A and 1) where the horizontal support level was tested again but it failed to break below it.

After the failure, price started moving higher, and there were evidence that bigger buyers were present as soon as you saw long bodied and short tailed trend bars (bar 2). The final confirmation was when price broke above Point B (bar 3 and 4).

6.4 Final Test of the Extremes

Before we explore the final test of the extremes, let's head back to the basic idea of reversion to mean that was discussed in Section 4.3.

Market Extremes

One of the beautiful phenomena about the trading the market is that the market is driven by humans (or human behaviour) and humans are usually *resistant to changes* – this is especially true at market extremes. That's the same reason why the buyers and sellers often put up a good fight before accepting that the market conditions have changed.

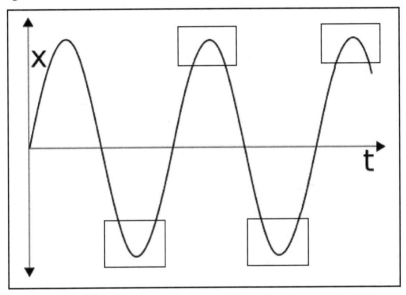

Diagram 6-9: Extreme Positions (Box) of a Pendulum Swing

In order to understand the concept of market extremes, let's use look at the pendulum again.

To begin with, we know that the pendulum swings from one side of the mean to another. At a certain point in time, it has to move away from the mean before it reaches an *extreme position* (the boxes in the diagram above). Then it reverses and swings towards the mean again.

If you believe that the extreme position is where the pendulum reverses, then you should also believe that the same happens in the financial market but it happens at *market extremes*. Unfortunately, the financial market is not as straight forward as the pendulum because no one knows where the market extreme is. Hence, the only way to find out is to constantly test the market until we reached the **Final Test**.

Final Test

Even though buyers and sellers are constantly testing the market, there will always be a dominant price leader when the market is trending. However, the test of the market (between the buyers and sellers) becomes more intense when they approach market extremes because it is at these extremes that the price leader changes from the buyers to sellers or vice versa.

Hence, the term **Final Test** represents the final attempt by the bulls or bears to push prices further before it reverses.

With that, here are some example scenarios when price is near market extremes.

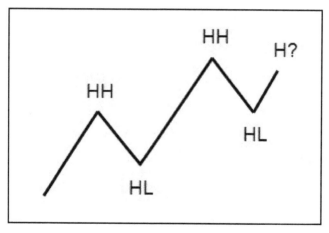

Diagram 6-10: Test of the Extremes

If you can, could you imagine a market that is at an extreme of a price cycle? Looking at the diagram above, imagine the market you are looking at is similar to it? Price is showing higher highs (HH) and higher lows (HL), which is a healthy indication of a bullish market.

Each time the market moves higher, there is a test of the last high because, for a new HH to exist, it needs to break and go beyond the last HH. These tests become more challenging as the market gets exhausted, and the number of buyers and sellers moves closer to equilibrium.

As you can see, the market made a recent HL and it begins to crawl higher again. With-trend traders would look for the break of the last HH again as a confirmation of a pullback. However, if the market shows signs of exhaustion, traders would be looking for those signs showing weakness and would stay out of the market until there is confirmation or even clues of reversal.

Essentially, any of the following could happen.

Lower High & Lower Low

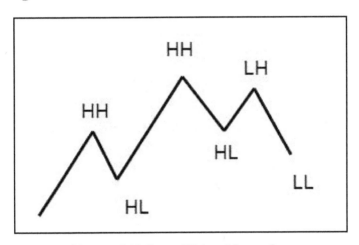

Diagram 6-11: Lower High and Lower Low

Working from Diagram 6-10, since the start of the last HL, price made a Lower High (LH) as this is where price failed to break above the last HH. This is followed by a Lower Low (LL) which is a confirmation that the LH is the final test. Just to be clear, the LH does not confirm the final test because you can still get a double bottom pullback and price could continue north. However, as soon as price made a LL, that was the confirmation that the pullback has failed.

Both the LH and LL are great clues showing the start of a downward trend. Also, this is a classic failed pullback pattern.

Double Top

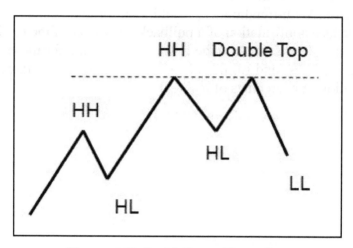

Diagram 6-12: Double Top and Lower Low

Alternatively, price could have made a clear final test when attempting to make a new high. However, on this occasion it didn't as it failed to break above the last HH. In fact, the failure made a double top instead. Similar to the previous scenario, a LL is required for confirmation of the final test. Without the LL, price could turn out to be a flat pullback, and it could end up moving sideways instead before making another test of last high.

A double top is a slightly earlier clue that the bulls are losing control and that the sellers are getting ready to enter the market. Because the double top is obvious to you, it means that other traders can spot it too. Hence, the likelihood that others would get into the trade has increased too – thus becoming a self-fulfilling prophecy.

Higher High & Lower Low

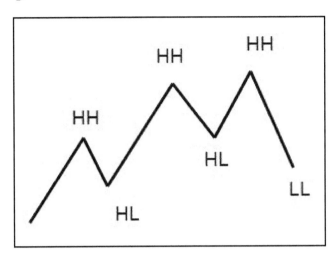

Diagram 6-13: Higher High and Lower Low

The diagram above shows another common test of the extreme. Price made the final test where it finished with a new HH. Nonetheless, the sellers came into the market and completely took control of price. While this usually traps the bulls, it is also a strong price action pattern showing commitment from the sellers who dominated the market. Smart buyers who see this would likely stay out of the market.

Due to the distance travelled from HH to LL, price would also likely have formed a bearish trend bar which is another good clue that the sellers are back. Essentially, the above is somewhat similar to an engulfing bar candlestick pattern if it was shown in a candlestick chart.

Higher High & Higher Low

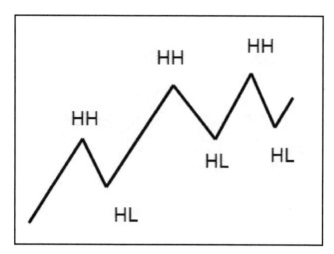

Diagram 6-14: Higher High and Higher Low

Lastly, it would not be surprising at all if price climbed higher to make another HH but this was followed by a HL. This only means that there are more tests to come, and this is *not* the final test yet. Essentially, this is back to square one and any of the above patterns could potentially happen either on the next test or anytime in the future.

6.5 Key Points

Here are the summaries and key pointers for this section:

- It is not surprising that pullbacks can fail. In fact, it is important that you know how and when they fail so that you are prepared for it.
- The failure of a failed pullback is equally important when trading pullbacks. Once you understand that, nothing can surprise you anymore.
- Understanding the final test of the extremes is to understand that buyers or sellers rarely give up easily. The examples showing the tests of the extreme shows the various scenarios of how market trends end and how they can continue further.

7 How to Use a Pullback?

Knowing what you know now about pullbacks, you should recognise that a pullback is a ***Price Action*** signal. Since most technical indicators are derived from price, by default, price is the only leading indicator in technical analysis. Above and beyond that, it is said that price action represents market and investors' behaviour. Hence, some would go to the extent to argue that price action incorporates fundamental analysis and macro information.

In other words, pullbacks are powerful indicators. With that, let's identify how this can be done.

7.1 Clues for Success

If you want to fully utilise pullbacks in your trading, it is worth understanding when and how a pullback can be profitable and, in order to achieve that, there are a few key areas that we need to establish before even considering taking any trades. One of the key areas that I'm referring to is market clues that are potentially signs of strength in price action.

You see, our objective as traders is to ***not*** predict the future. You may ask – "If we are not predicting the future, then how else are we going to make money from trading?"

With that, I would like to invite you to think of trading in terms of an exercise of stacking probabilities. Instead of trying to predict the future, we search for clues in order to stack the probability of success in our favour. Hence, the more clues we can find, the more likely that the pullback can work in our favour.

This section is about understanding the various clues for success in the market. I hope that by understanding these clues, you are able to stop predicting and to start collecting clues instead.

7.1.1 Depth of a pullback

The depth of a pullback is one of the easiest and straight forward methods of identifying the strength of a pullback.

Shallow Vs Deep Pullbacks

In Section 5.2.1, we've outlined some of the characteristics of shallow pullbacks and one of the characteristics is that it is likely to be a one-sided market. That just means, in an up market, buyers are dominating the battle and, in a down market, sellers are the dominant ones.

Since the market is one-sided in a shallow pullback, only a few investors push the price against the DTD. The chances are high that the trend would remain strong for awhile. Hence, as soon as the pullback is completed, the market will be waiting eagerly to continue its push further.

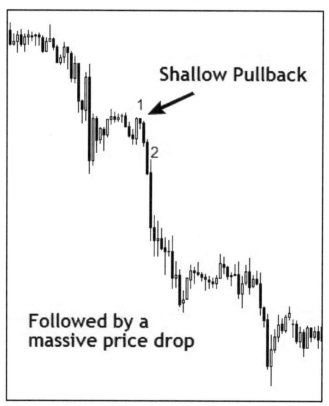

Diagram 7-1: Shallow Pullback Shows Strength

Secrets of Trading the First Pullback

Looking at the diagram above, the buyers tried to push the price higher (bar 1 near the arrow). However, they didn't have the resources to do so. On the other hand, sellers did not wait long before they sold the market again and that formed a shallow pullback.

The shallow pullback was a good sign that the sellers were in control and they continued to push price even lower. While we don't have external data with us here, price action was showed strong seller trend bars (bar 2) and these were confirmations that the sellers had the control over the market.

Also, once the market started moving again, smart buyers who saw such momentum will stay out of the market. Hence, it is self fulfilling that with little or no buyers, the market can only move in one direction and would do so easily.

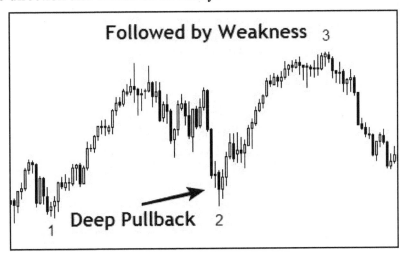

Diagram 7-2: Deep Pullback Shows Weakness

The opposite is also true. A deep pullback often leads to less aggressive price movements at the end of the pullback. The above example shows a very deep pullback (bar2) and price had gone quite close to the start of the previous low (bar 1) before it resumed its move in the DTD. However, as you can see, price did not move far before it showed signs of weakness and it started its move down

www.MarketApprentice.com

again. As you can see, the bulls did not show conviction anymore and there is little strength in pushing the price higher (bar 3 was the next high).

As mentioned in Section 6.4, as you get close to the market extremes, this is when buyers and sellers move towards equilibrium. In case you haven't realised, deep pullbacks also provide similar clues. Hence, deep pullbacks can sometimes be a good indication that the market is nearly exhausted, and the trend could end soon.

A Mechanical Approach

A more mechanical approach to measuring pullback can be done by using the Fib Ret tool. As shown in Section 5.4, it is common to find a pullback arriving at a specific Fib Ret ratio before price resumes back into the DTD.

The ratios that are good indicators of a shallow pullback are 23.6% and 38.2%. On the other hand, 61.8% and 76.4% are considered having deep or deeper pullbacks.

In other words, if you find a pullback reversing around 23.6% or 38.2% Fib ratio, these are pullbacks that could potentially indicate that price can go much further. If you find pullbacks reversing around 61.8% and 76.4% ratios, the chances are higher that they can show weakness.

Secrets of Trading the First Pullback

Diagram 7-3: S&P500 Index showing Strong Selling Pressure

The hourly chart of the S&P500 Index showed a pullback retracing up to 38.2% Fib ratio (circled) before price continued its trend downwards. As shown above, there was a gap when the market opened but that did not affect how price reacted to the 38.2% level where it turned around and resumed its original move.

After the initial pullback, price continues to drop and you could find more pullbacks along the way. As a trader, do not panic as it is normal for price to continue to retrace time and again. In fact, these pullbacks go deeper and deeper as more and more buyers gradually enter the market causing the downward momentum to lose its strength.

www.MarketApprentice.com

Secrets of Trading the First Pullback

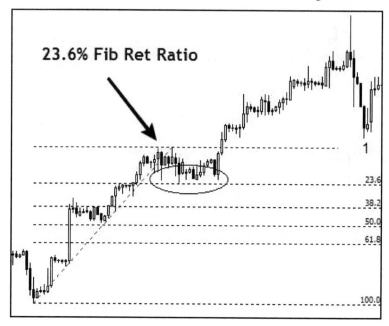

Diagram 7-4: AUDUSD Pair showing Strong Buying Pressure

The AUDUSD currency pair showed a shallow retracement on the 15 minute chart (circled). The flat pullback around the 23.6% Fib ratio continued to push higher. Again, price started to make deeper pullbacks and the sharp pullback (bar 1) is a good example of that. Knowing that there is strength in the market, smart buyers see the sharp pullback as a good buying opportunity to buy at a cheaper price before price climbs higher.

Secrets of Trading the First Pullback

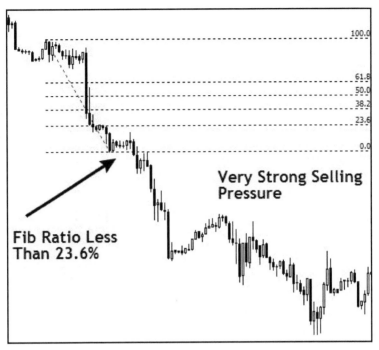

Diagram 7-5: Dow Jones Index showing Strong Selling Pressure

The next diagram, Dow Jones Index on the 15 minute chart, depicts a retracement that has a pullback ratio that is less than 23.6%. While it might be difficult to spot these pullbacks in a live market, it just goes to show that these types of pullback are great indicators for strong selling pressure.

Of course, it's easier to look at a chart and the market in hindsight. However, you need to practice spotting shallow pullbacks before you can take advantage of them. It is important to make an effort to search and to recognise these pullbacks as they are great set ups. The one-sided market will tilt the bias in our favour.

7.1.2 Trend Bars

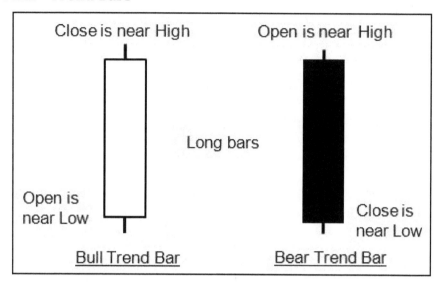

Diagram 7-6: Buyer and Seller Trend Bars

Trend bars or Marubozu price action bars have often been underrated by technical traders because many seem to be looking for technical indicators instead. Hence, I would like to highlight the fact that trend bars are great to show strengths in the market, and you should look for them especially *at the start of a new trend*. They are very useful clues for trading success especially near extremes.

Essentially, trend bars are impulse price action which indicates that the big players are driving the market. Big players usually have deep pockets to push the market, and they do so in the medium to long term. Hence, the longer the trend bars the better.

If the trend bar is longer than the average size bar, that is also a good indication of *momentum* and this is usually the start of a market rally (or decline). If you find that the trend bars have very small tails that is evidence that the market is one-sided, and the momentum is increased further.

Secrets of Trading the First Pullback

Alternatively, if the trend bar is at the end of the run, this can be an indication of *exhaustion*.

Definition of Trend Bar
  The Long Buyer Trend bar has short tails including:
  - Close near High
  - Open near Low
  The Long Seller Trend bar has short tails including:
  - Close near Low
  - Open near High

Diagram 7-7: Gold Showing Sellers' Conviction

www.MarketApprentice.com

Secrets of Trading the First Pullback

In the Gold 4 hour chart above, the sellers showed conviction as soon as the first trend bar closed (bar 1). The bar was long and had short tails. The length of the bar was multiples of its preceding bars (not shown), and it shows that the sellers were serious.

After the initial trend bar, price made a double top pullback (circled) before it presented another trend bar (bar 3).

Smart sellers would have taken a short entry at that double top pullback. Meanwhile, those who wanted more confirmation may have taken the break below bar 2 as soon as the pullback was completed. Alternative, more short positions would have been taken at the shallow pullback immediately after bar 3.

Diagram 7-8: FTSE Index Showing Buyers Conviction

www.MarketApprentice.com

The FTSE Index on the daily chart (above) started off with three buyer bars with the centre one being a trend bar (bar 1). The Japanese calls the three candlesticks a *Three Advancing White Soldiers*.

While that was a bullish pattern, the next bullish clue was a simple and sharp pullback (circled) at a 38.2% Fib Ret ratio that finished with a long buyer trend bar with small tails. The combination of factors showed plenty of reasons that the bulls were serious, the subsequent run after that was just further confirmation as price barely made any more pullbacks until later.

7.1.3   Horizontal Support & Resistance Levels

Price action horizontal support and resistance is a simple yet powerful clue to use when searching for areas where a pullback could reverse back into the DTD. This is also considered more reliable because the horizontal levels are less subjective compared to other clues since each support or resistance only require one piece of information – a swing high or swing low.

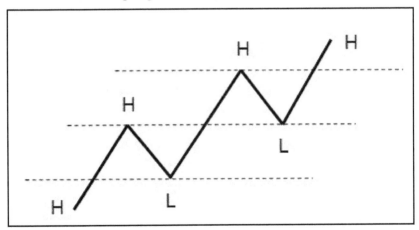

Diagram 7-9: Creating Support and Resistance Levels

Using the diagram above as an example, you can see that each swing high (H) was identified as a horizontal resistance level. Once price broke above that level, price would then retest the swing high where the resistance could turn support.

In other words, more often than not, prices are reacting to the price swings created in the past. While each H and L could be new in the existing cycle, some of them could coincide with past swing Hs and Ls.

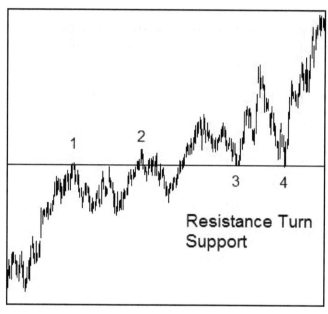

Diagram 7-10: Hammerson PLC (Daily Chart) Showing Resistance and Support Levels

Looking at the Hammerson PLC (Daily Chart) above, price made a swing high at bar 1 and made a higher high at bar 2. Nonetheless, price consolidated around bar 2 before it made a swing low and a new high after it broke above bar 1 and bar 2.

Bar 3 was a good retest of bar 1 swing high, and it turned out to be a good bounce back into the DTD. Interestingly, price came back down again to test that same level (bar 4) and it eventually became a double bottom pullback.

7.1.4 Knowing the Market Players and Timeframe

Understanding timeframe correlation is probably one of the most important knowledge in any technical trading. However, before I dive into the subject of timeframe correlation, it might be worth grasping the relationship between timeframe and market players.

Market Players

There are various market players in the financial market and they each have a different role to play in the market. Due to the varying objectives that they carry with them when they enter the market, they influence the market differently.

For simplicity, I have grouped the various market players in three categories (below). I have also included a short summary of characteristics of the respective players:

Big Players

- Central banks or major financial institutions
- They are long term market players and usually drive the markets as they have deep pockets.
- They usually enter the market for fundamental reasons only.
- They usually enter the market on a **larger** timeframe.

Mid Players

- Mid-sized or small-sized banks, large hedge funds, market makers, large corporate or commercial companies
- A mixture of short term and long term players. However, they are usually able to influence the small players.
- They enter the market for fundamental **and** profit making objectives.
- They usually enter the market on **any** timeframe.

Small Players

- Retail and private individual traders.

- They have little influence over the market.
- They usually have profit making objectives only.
- They usually enter the market on *any* timeframe.

The Bigger Picture

As you can see, understanding the market players can potentially help you plan ahead because you cannot ignore the fact that they are able to influence other market players, as well as the direction of market trend.

In order to further elaborate my point, here are two obvious relationships between the market players and timeframe. I hope to highlight the importance of the bigger picture.

Strong Trending Day Bars

If you see long trend bars on a daily or weekly chart, especially at the start of the new trend, be prepared for a strong trending market. As mentioned previously, strong trend bars are good indication of strength but a trend bar on a bigger timeframe is more reliable than one in an intraday timeframe.

As stated earlier, the big players are in the market for the longer term. When they enter the market, they have the resources to fuel the movement of price in a certain direction for a relatively long time. Above that, they enter the market in small chunks – as oppose to putting their entire buy or sell orders in one trade.

Hence, when you see a strong trend bar on the daily chart (or even on the 8 hour charts), be ready to follow that same direction because that is usually a good indication that the big players are in the market. In fact, all you need to do is to follow them and the probability of winning increases as well.

Aimless Market

Secrets of Trading the First Pullback

If you are a short term trend trader and you're facing an aimless market, you may find that you are constantly being kicked out of your trade. While you are certain that you are following your rules, you feel that the market is against you.

Guess what? You're probably right. These are the days that you should be cautious because – and it's not that the entire market is against you but – the chances are that the mid players (e.g. hedge fund traders) are manipulating the market in order to meet their daily profit targets.

This usually happens when the market (on the larger timeframe) is consolidating. Remember that a consolidation is when the market is undecided. This is also a period when mid-players take control as they know that the big players are probably sitting out. At this stage, the big players probably have most (or all) their orders filled and they are waiting aside until they decide to either push the market further or to exit it.

Also, since the objective of mid players (which includes market makers) are purely financial (i.e. profit making), that means they can use of any trading systems as long as it's profitable. With that, you can probably see why the word "manipulate" is a good representation of the mid players.

However, the only real thing that we know about mid players is that they lose their control of the market when the big players are back into the market. Again, these are usually obvious on larger timeframes.

As you can see, the above are illustrations of two extreme market conditions. The truth is that the financial market usually goes through either of the above or experiences something in between at any point in time. That is also what determines a trending, reversal and ranging market.

The real challenge is that we don't know what happens next. However, if you are uncertain about the market conditions, always use a larger timeframe for clues. For example, if you are trading a 5 minute chart, it will be worth checking on the 60 minute chart for direction. If you are trading a 4 hour chart, it is be worth checking the daily chart etc. Hope that makes sense?

Looking for the right market players can be somewhat challenging but, do not be despair, because all you need is practice. More importantly, when probability works in our favour, price action usually shows sign of strengths that can help us find those winning trades.

7.2 Key Points

Here are the summaries and key pointers for this section:

- Price action is a leading indicator and, hence, price pullback is a great price action tool.
- In order to increase the chances of trading success in a trending market, you should look out for clues to increase the probability of success. These clues include:
    - Shallow Pullbacks
    - Trend Bars
    - Price Channels
    - Horizontal Support and Resistance level
    - Knowing the market players and timeframe

8 The Best Pullback

If you have been following the book from the start, I believe you should have had a decent understanding of what a price action pullback is all about by now. If you have, then let's try to dive into a little more detail.

Since pullbacks are everywhere, you need to appreciate the fact that some pullbacks have higher chances of success than the others. Hence, in this section, I hope to share some ideas on ways to pick pullbacks that could yield better probabilities of success.

8.1 Next Best Entry

If you want to be profitable trading market pullbacks, let it be no secret that the best pullback is the *First* pullback. The first pullbacks are the with-trend entries that can be found at the very start of a new trend.

With that, let's explore the idea of trading the first pullbacks.

Secrets of Trading the First Pullback

Diagram 8-1: Ideal Top and Bottom Entries

In an ideal situation, the most profitable way to trade the market is to catch the run from the very top and cash out at the bottom of the market. The opposite is also true if you catch it from the bottom and exit right at the top of the market. However, the nature of trading is such that we never really know where the top or bottom is. Above and beyond that, catching the top or the bottom of the market is probably one of the harder tasks and many traders have lost substantial amount of money while attempting to do so.

Secrets of Trading the First Pullback

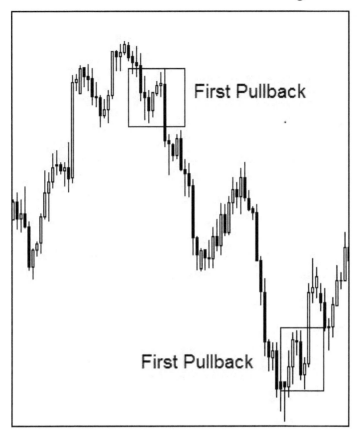

Diagram 8-2: Near Top and Bottom Entries

Instead of entering the market at the top or bottom, the first pullback allows traders to enter *near* the top or bottom (as shown in the box above), this is somewhat similar to entering at the top or bottom, and you can still enjoy the majority of the benefits. Hence, entering the market at the first pullback is the ***next best entry***.

Essentially, the first pullback *in the new trend direction* is also the final test of the extreme *in the old trend direction*. Hence, understanding the final test of the extreme is fairly important when identifying the first pullback. It is also the failed test because it failed to make a new extreme.

www.MarketApprentice.com

Just to be clear, the first pullback is not a reversal set up. Instead, it is a with-trend setup that enters the market at a very early stage of the new trend – it is the *first with-trend entry immediately after price has reversed*. Sometimes, one would be in the market while others wait for confirmation.

However, while many would be afraid to enter the market, smart traders understand that this is a low risk and high reward set up. In fact, it is a great and safe entry. Of course, it is also important that you have sufficient **Clues for Success** before taking a position, where we will go through in more detail.

8.2 First Pullback in New Direction

As we know, when the trend ends, it does not imply that the new trend would start immediately. Hence, it is crucial that you need to know what price action clues to look for when looking for the first pullbacks.

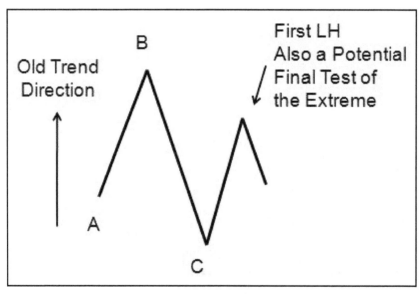

Diagram 8-3: Testing the Extreme in Old Direction

Before we search for the first pullback, I think it's worth talking about price action right before it happens.

Secrets of Trading the First Pullback

Using the example above, the market is currently in an uptrend (old trend direction). The first indication of a potential new pullback (in a new direction) is when you see the first LH. This is because the LH is a sign of weakness that is shows that the buyers are not completely in control.

As discussed earlier, this is also a potential final test of the extreme high. Buyers are testing to see if they can move any higher. Meanwhile, the sellers are keeping a close eye, once they know that buyers are exhausted, big sellers would take control of the market, and they would push price lower. However, the confirmation of the final test requires a LL or, in this case, a break below Point C.

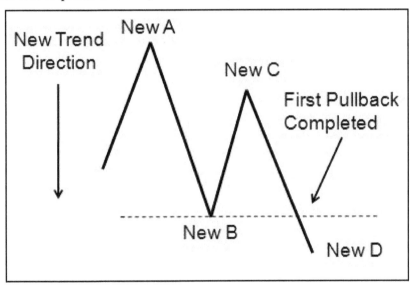

Diagram 8-4: First Pullback in New Direction

When you have a LH (the New C in the diagram above) and when price breaks below Point C (the New B in diagram above), the interesting part about price action is that it is also where the first pullback in new direction is completed.

In other words, you can then find a new ABCD in the new direction.

In case you have forgotten (as mentioned in Section 5.1), BC is the actual pullback but *a pullback must include CD* where D moves beyond B or the pullback is invalid. The same applies here and, hence, price must move below the New B for confirmation of ***the first pullback in the new trend direction***.

Once you have a full cycle, the chances are higher that the market is now in a downtrend, and the chances are now slimmer for price to move upwards or sideways since the downward market has already started.

8.3 Combining Clues for First Pullbacks

So that was it. The first pullback is now on the way. However, understanding the first pullback means nothing if you do not take any positions. You either catch the new pullback or you missed it. Truth to be told, there is nothing much you can do about it once you miss a run.

As you can see, trading is about preparation and the more you are prepared for it, the more you can grab a high probability trade. Hence, this section helps identify the clues for success for catching the first pullback.

We did discuss the clues for success in Section 7.1 and some of those clues are applicable here as well. However, as we continue to dig deeper into the nature of the first pullback, I will share some simple ways where you can combine certain clues to achieving even higher probabilities of success.

8.3.1 Conviction of a Failed Pullback

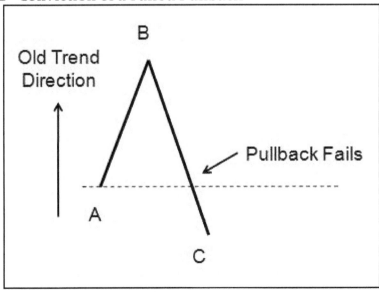

Diagram 8-5: Pullback Fails in Old Direction

Secrets of Trading the First Pullback

Here's a quick reminder of how pullbacks fail. Looking at the diagram above, we can see that price break below Pt A and that is a confirmation that the pullback has failed. This is also the first LL that we were looking for.

While we don't know what happens next, we can only wait for more price confirmation to show us if the buyers or sellers are taking the lead. Nonetheless, the only thing that we are certain is the old trend has lost its drive and that is an important clue to note.

See Section 6.2 for details of failed pullbacks.

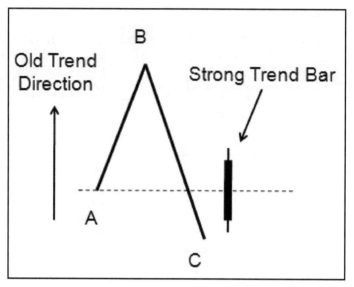

Diagram 8-6: Trend Bar showing confirmation of Failed Pullback

While a failed pullback is important, we need the probabilities to stack in our favour. Hence, in terms of price action, you want to see a *clear break* below Point A and one of the best ways to identify seller's conviction is by finding one or more long bodied bearish trend bar breaking through point A.

This is a strong confirmation that the pullback has failed and the probability of getting a failure of a failed pullback has greatly reduced.

See Section 7.1.2 for details of trend bars.

8.3.2   Spotting Big Players at Market Extremes

Market extremes, relates to the fact that price is pretty far from average or mean price. As mentioned in Section 6.4, the final test of the market extreme is a good indication that the old trend is ending and, hence, it is useful in picking up potential pullbacks in the new trend directions.

However, to maximise a pullback at a price extreme, traders should try their best to understand timeframe correlation because, sometimes, the patterns are only obvious at relevant timeframes – usually the larger one.

For example:

- A price extreme at the 60 minute chart is more relevant when trading a 15 minute chart
- A price extreme at the daily chart is more relevant when trading a 60 minute or 4 hourly chart
- A price extreme at the weekly chart is more relevant when trading daily chart

Just to be clear, the timeframe of your analysis shows where the big players are heading. Meanwhile, the timeframe below that shows you the pattern or pullback that you are looking. Although this might not always be the case, the probability of success increases once you master the ability to spot the big players (using timeframe management).

www.MarketApprentice.com

Secrets of Trading the First Pullback

Diagram 8-7: Silver showing Market Extreme on Daily Chart

Looking at Silver in the diagram above, you can see from the daily chart that price was very far away from the moving average line. Price stayed far away from the line and even climaxed (boxed) at the top. That was considered the extreme since it was at the point where it was furthest away from the average line (red line).

However, there was no clue showing the lack of buyers until we saw the first lower high in the 4 hour.

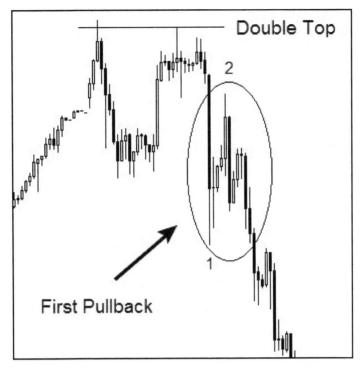

Diagram 8-8: Silver showing First Pullback on 4 Hour chart near Daily Extreme

Using the daily chart to identify the market extreme as your clue, you can then move to the 4 hour chart to pinpoint when price pullback fails in the initial trend direction. The diagram above is the box found in Diagram 8-7.

As you can see, the first clue that the buyers have run out of strength is the price action double top – a final test of the extreme. Then, it was followed by a LL (bar 1) as well as a LH (bar 2). The confirmation of the first pullback (circled) in the new trend direction was when price broke below bar 1.

If you stayed on the daily timeframe, you might not have spotted the pullback and would have missed a good pullback entry.

8.4 Other Forms of First Pullbacks

I hope the descriptions of the first pullback have been reasonably clear. The first pullback is one of the best pullbacks in a price action setup and traders should learn to identify them where ever possible.

On that note, here are more examples of price action pullbacks which can be found in different patterns. As I am an advocate of trading price action, I would encourage you to understand why the following setups are good *in relation to pullbacks* and I hope it does not turn out to be an exercise of merely memorising the patterns.

8.4.1 Reversal Patterns

Since a first pullback is an early entry in a new trend, it should be no surprise that you can find many first pullbacks immediately after a reversal pattern. Hence, I believe it is worth exploring some conventional reversal patterns. Just to be clear, as with-trend traders, the idea is not to trade the reversal patterns and it is important to wait for price to have *reversed* before looking for any first pullback entry.

On a separate note, there is nothing wrong with taking a reversal trade based on reversal set ups. However, this book is about trading *with the trend*, and it should be clear that these reversal patterns are only used as clues rather then set ups.

Here are examples to illustrate how one can trade the first pullback in reversal price patterns.

Double Top/Bottom and Neckline Pullback

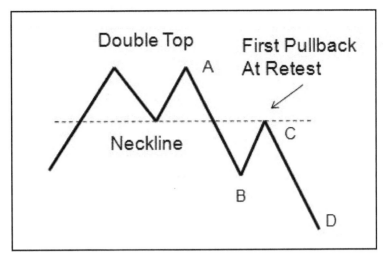

Diagram 8-9: Double Top Neckline Pullback

As shown above, a double top pattern is a good and simple indication that the price has tested the extreme one last time and resulted in a final test, in the old trend direction.

However, as a with-trend trader, the double top is only a potential start of a new pullback (A) and the clues that you should be looking for are the new lower low (B) and a new lower high (C).

The *retest of the neckline* is an extra but powerful clue as it is where the old support becomes resistance. In other words, the double top is only the first clue, but not a confirmation that a first pullback is ready.

A double bottom would act in a similar but opposite fashion.

Range Market Breakouts

A range market can happen around the market extreme or in the middle of a trending market. It is pretty important that the trader should identify the *bigger players* (as discussed in Section 8.3.2) before having a market bias.

Secrets of Trading the First Pullback

As you are aware, a range market is only formed if there are 2 touches on either side of the market (this is required to form the *ceiling* and the *floor*) and these are important clues to confirm a range market.

A range market can be somewhat tricky. Hence, if you're not certain of the clues, it might be worth keeping a log of it for a few times before acting on it. Once you have a range market, watch out for failed or false breakouts. Unless you are a range or breakout trader, with-trend traders usually stay aside until we get sufficient price action clues.

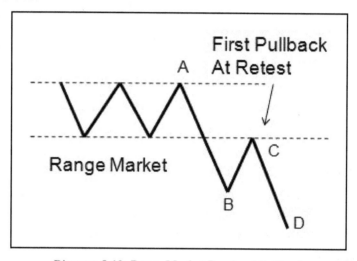

Diagram 8-10: Range Market Breakout Pullback

As you can see from the diagram above, Point B is the first lower low, and it is also the first break outside the range. However, B can also be a false break, and you can only find out if it is by watching C and D closely.

Point C is the first lower high and also a retest of the resistance (previous support) level. Like all other pullbacks, the first pullback is only complete once we have D, which is the break below B to form a second lower low and also a complete ABCD pattern.

If this was at a market extreme, point A could potentially act like a double (or triple) top which is also the final test of the extreme. On the other hand, if the market was in a downward trend, then point A could be a double top bearish continuation pullback pattern.

Either way, do not get too bogged down with the terminologies because, if you do, the chances are high that you can miss lots of profitable trades. Instead, read price action carefully and understand the bigger picture. When price changes from a sideways market to a trending market, the consolidation market acts as a spring where investors are ready to burst out after a period of indecision.

H&S Neckline

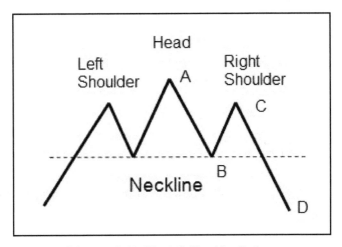

Diagram 8-11: Head & Shoulder Pattern

The Head & Shoulder (H&S) pattern is a classic triple top pattern and, like a double top, it is also a good sign of price exhaustion.

As shown above, an H&S pattern would consist of three tops where the left shoulder is the first top, the head is the second (and highest) top and the right shoulder is the third top. The two lows in between the three tops would determine the shape of the neckline – as it can be a *horizontal* or a *slope* neckline.

In a horizontal neckline, the entire H&S pattern relies on the fact that D must be below B, which is also below the neckline. With that, the neckline carries quite a bit of probability weight. If price fails to break below the neckline, this could turn out to be a double (or even triple) bottom bullish continuation pullback.

Elliot Wave

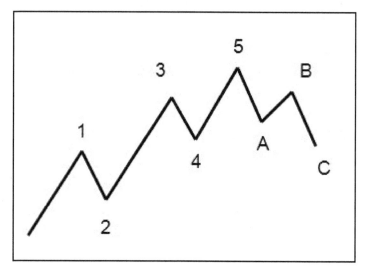

Diagram 8-12: Elliot Wave Theory

The Elliot Wave Theory is a technical analysis tool developed by R.N. Elliott and the theory suggests that the basic wave principles can be divided into two main categories –Impulse and Corrective waves.

According to the theory, here are some key rules that R.N. Elliot developed:

- Impulse waves has a 5-wave sequence (wave 1-5 – see above)

- A 3-wave corrective sequence (wave ABC – see above) follows after the impulse wave ends.
- Wave 2 cannot retrace beyond wave 1
- Wave 3 is the longest amongst all the impulse waves (wave 1,3 and 5)
- Wave 4 can never overlap wave 1

As you can see, according to the Elliot Wave theory, catching first pullback in the impulse wave happens to be the most profitable setup since wave 3 is the mother (longest) of all waves. On the other hand, the first 5 waves serves as a clue in preparation for the first pullback in the opposition direction and that is wave C in the corrective wave sequence.

Note:

These are just brief extracts of Elliot Wave Theory to show that the first pullback can be applied and is inline with the Elliot Waves. However, this section is not designed to teach or explain the use of Elliot Wave Theory.

8.5 Key Points

Here are the summaries and key pointers for this section:

- The best pullback is the first pullback in the new trend direction. Since it is difficult to pick tops and bottoms, trading the first pullback provides setups that are near tops and bottoms.
- Clues become more powerful when you start combining more than one of them. The two main combination discussed in this section includes
    - Identifying convicted failed pullback
    - Identifying big players at market extremes
- Reversal patterns are great signals in advance of the first pullback. Hence, it is useful to know them. However, learn to pick up clues for success in those patterns.

9 Building a Case

9.1 Stacking Probabilities

Double Top Neckline Pullback

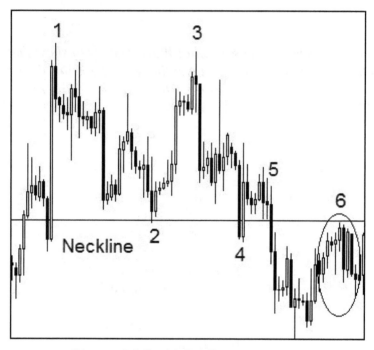

Diagram 9-1: Double Top Neckline Pullback

The diagram above shows the EURUSD 60 minute chart. Bar 1 and 3 shows a double top pattern before price started moving south. That was also a good enough indication for price reversal. Bar 2 was a good level to draw the neckline because that was the prior low before the double top (Bar 1 and 3).

Meanwhile, while bar 4 seems like a false breakout initially (as a false breakout can happen in similar situations). However, bar 5 showed sellers' conviction as the long trend bar pushed price below the neckline and below bar 4 with certainty. It also formed a convincing lower low.

Secrets of Trading the First Pullback

Once bar 5 gave the confirmation of the lower low, traders would wait for the first pullback after the lower high and the retest of the neckline at bar 6.

Range Market Breakouts

Diagram 9-2: Range Market Breakout Pullback

The above is the EURUSD currency pair on a 4 hour chart. As you can see, bar 1 & 3 formed the ceiling of the range market and bar 2 & 4 formed the floor.

Since this was a market extreme on a daily or weekly chart (not shown), this would have been a good place for sellers to wait for the first pullback in the new direction. Buyers who did not spot that would have placed their orders slightly above bar 1 for a double bottom pullback but their orders would not have been filled.

www.MarketApprentice.com

The first clue of a short was when bar 5 broke below the floor and bar 4, that was also a nice trend bar showing some conviction. Breakout traders would have taken the short at bar 5, but with-trend traders would have waited for the first pullback (in case bar 5 turned into a false break).

Bar 6 was a failed false breakout – since the buyers attempted to push price higher back into the range before the sellers took charge to send price back out of the range again. Trend traders would view this as a failure of a failed pullback in the new direction.

Irrespective of what the pattern was called, the market players were trying to outsmart each other by testing the market on both directions. Fortunately, the sellers took the final control of the market at bar 6 and pushed price below bar 5, and that was the confirmation of the first pullback.

H&S Pattern

Head & Shoulder (H&S) patterns are fairly challenging to spot, and it's usually easier in hindsight. However, one can expect it to appear if it is near the extreme.

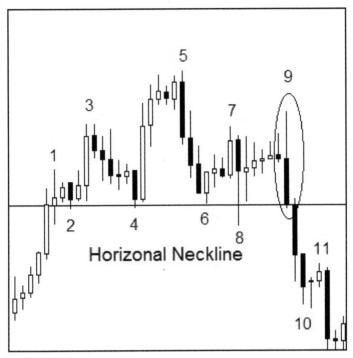

Diagram 9-3: GBPUSD (4 Hour chart) shows H&S Pattern with Horizontal Neckline

The above is one chart that would have kicked new traders out of the market for a variety of reasons. Looking at the chart, bar 2 would have been a decent flat pullback but with-trend traders would be too eager to enter at bar 2. Instead, a break above bar 1 would have been a safe entry – which it did at bar 3.

Bar 3 was a Trend bar, and it was the first confirmation of the flat pullback. Unfortunately, price did not follow through. When you see that the bulls have not followed through after bar 3, traders should be careful that as this is the first sign of buyers' weakness. It was also a good clue that would lead to a potential complex pullback or even a failed pullback.

Through the use of a smaller timeframe, some would argue that Bar 4 tested the low of bar 2 and they formed a double bottom. That became a double bottom pullback as soon as price broke above bar 3. However, based on the timeframe that is shown above, that was not obvious enough and we can just assume that it was only a simple pullback pattern.

The trend bar after bar 4 was another indication that the buyers want to take control. However, it did not take long before we saw price consolidating and bar 5 was the confirmation that the sellers were strong too – a bearish trend bar which is also an engulfing bar. The buyers came back for the 3rd time at bar 6.

At this stage, *it was clear that the market had no dominant leader* and buyers/ sellers were equally strong. Smart traders would be extra cautious from here on.

As soon as bar 7 made a new high (though it was not above bar 5), it was clear that bar 4 and 6 had made a double bottom. In fact, since they were at similar price level, the double bottom formed a decent horizontal support.

Bar 8 broke below the support level but failed to hold on below it. This was a test of the level, and it was also a confirmation that the support held on well at that price level. Some buyers were excited as this was also a reasonable indication that the buyers were in control. However, while this could be an early clue, the confirmation of a trend continuation only happens when price breaks above bar 5 and that is when price shows a new higher high – unfortunately, that did not happen.

After bar 8, the string of doji bars was another confirmation that neither the buyers nor sellers were in control. As those doji bars formed a small range market, breakout traders would have taken the break above bar 7 as a setup but that turned out to be a false break. Sellers jumped into it as soon as it failed and pushed price further down from bar 9. From that point onwards, price just went lower and lower.

Sellers' showed conviction when price broke below the double bottom support level as well as below bar 8. On top of that, the low of Bar 8 was where buyers placed their protective stops (which were sell orders). As soon as price went below bar 8, those protective stops got triggered in and fuelled the bearish move even further.

Both bar 7 and 9 were tests of the extreme (which was the high of bar 5), where bar 9 was the final test. The move from bar 8 to 9 was the first pullback, but there was no confirmation until price went below bar 8.

Unfortunately, this was a complex pullback within an H&S pattern – with bar 3 as the left shoulder, bar 5 as the head and bar 9 as the right shoulder. In fact, the H&S pattern was not confirmed until it reached bar 10.

With so much indecision, the highest probability trade was at the break below the neckline. Alternatively, traders would have taken the break below bar 8 since that was the new lower low and that as also the first pullback in the new direction. New traders would have been trapped if they had entered when price went below bar 6 and they would have stayed away.

The next pullback after that was at bar 11. This was a shallow pullback after the confirmation of the H&S pattern.

www.MarketApprentice.com

9.2 Key Points

Here are the summaries and key pointers for this section:

- Before you take the first pullback, constantly look for clues that would support your decision. The more clues you have, the better chances of success.
- When there is no clear leader in the price action war, it's always best to stay out of the market.
- First pullbacks are high probability trades. However, there is no guarantee that the first pullback always win. All you know is that it can be profitable in the long term if you trade with multiple clues for success.

10 Mastery – What's That All About?

"A person has "mastered" a particular area of skill when he or she is able to have both conscious and unconscious competence with respect to that skill.

Let's take for example a wood carver. Knowing the techniques of being a good wood carver may make a person a good technician, but does not necessarily make a person a "master". In this sense, mastery can be contrasted with technical "competency." In addition to behavioural competence, the master knows the rules of wood carving, the elements that guide the rules, and has intuitions about what is well-formed in the process of carving wood. Mastery can also be contrasted with artistry (the next level beyond mastery) which, according to Gregory Bateson, is the process of "bending the rules" in a well-formed way. The master is someone who is beyond being a technician and well on his or her way towards artistry."

– NLPU

Mastery, for a market trader, goes beyond technical know-how and monetary achievements. Of course, majority of traders I know are in it for the money initially. However, as you continue to achieve your financial goals, trading becomes more than just wealth achievements. For many, it becomes part of their livelihood, and they feel rather uncomfortable not staying in touch with the market.

If you truly want to become successful in trading, I strongly urge that you to work towards trading mastery – as opposed to having wealth objectives *only*. Learning to trade the market requires your commitment that goes beyond wealth because once you are a master at it, achieving wealth is easy and effortless.

Above and beyond that, don't just take what I say or wrote. In fact, challenge everything that I wrote in this book, because unless you do that, achieving mastery is just another fancy word that you just read. A good wood carver started off by getting his/her hands dirty before knowing what rules are relevant and what rules are not. Because he/she has practiced the skills so many times, he/she is able to apply all the rules easily and effortless, and that was when bending the rules became possible.

I believe some useful pointers can help you go a long way and that is what this section is about. The following are some areas which is important to achieving trading mastery.

10.1 Four Steps to Mastery

I won't be surprised that some of you would start applying the technical setups in the market immediately. In fact, I hope you do, because the faster you start applying it, the faster you can start making money.

Nonetheless, mastery is a journey. More than that, you also know that achieving mastery would require the trader to apply the same skills over and over again. This is the simple idea of ***repetition*** works because each time you harness the same skills, you apply those skills better than the last time you did it. Essentially, it is the repetition that helps you become competent.

While it is not crucial to know these steps, knowing it is half the battle. I have met many impatient traders who neither appreciate nor understand the importance of repetition. However, reading this right now, you know you can stand out successfully to be a winner. In order to help you understand the road to mastery, I hope the following steps are useful.

Unconscious Incompetence

> Remember the first time you open a chart, you realised that it seems like seeing a bunch of lines with fancy colours, and nothing make sense to you.
>
> This is where most of us started our trading career as complete amateurs. You ventured into the trading world hoping to gain new wealth, and you may (or may not) have sought after various resources in the hope of learning how to trade. At this stage, you were clueless as to what resources were useful and what were not.

Some of you would have invested in trading courses while some have relied on books and published materials.

Either way, in this first stage of trading, *you don't know what you don't know*.

Conscious Incompetence

Once you've collected your resources, you start to learn simple price action or trading systems. Some of you would have learned specific skills if you joined a course. However, most of you are still confused when you see a chart full of candlesticks or bars.

While you start to learn the building blocks of price charts, you struggled to make any sense out of it.

As you continue to acquire new knowledge, you start to fluctuate between being **unconscious incompetence** and **conscious incompetence**. Each time you learn a new tool and try to apply it in the market, you realise that there is a gap in knowledge, or you may find that there is '*something*' lacking. You then get back to your 'library' in the hope of finding more resources to learn more.

This is the stage where traders are most curious and, here, you can expect a steep learning curve. This is also the most challenging stage as it is can be the most emotional (for some). The impatient ones are eager to start using real money. Unfortunately, most of them lose it. Don't be despair because there is always confusion right before any growth.

At this stage, *you know what you don't know*.

Conscious Competence

This where the real trading development begins because, at this stage, you have learned **enough**. By enough, I mean there is sufficient knowledge inside you to keep yourself going, and you consciously choose to stop learning until necessary. In fact, you start to revisit all the lessons that you've had or kept throughout your training in the hope of filling any gaps that you may have.

More importantly, you suddenly realise that you have clarity over all the work that you've done since you first started trading. You understand what you did wrong and right, you start to appreciate that trading is a probability game, you recognise the importance of following the process and you learn to stop chasing trades. These are only some of the signs that you are now consciously picked up.

While you may make some occasional mistakes, you are now aware and conscious of what is required to be a successful trader. Hence, you work towards your beliefs, and *you start to apply what you know*.

Unconscious Competence

As soon you get pass the previous stage, the final stage is like driving a car with years of driving experience (assuming you drive a car on a daily basis). Everything you do – from putting on your seat belt to using your left or right indicators, and from pressing on the breaks to the accelerator – they are now performed at an unconscious level. Most of the time, you don't even remember what you did when prompted because it is now a habit.

This is where you know you are unconsciously competent.

For traders, you want to be able to place a trade without second guessing yourself. You are managing your trades without having to debate internally what you are about to do. Making a decision to trade is *effortless*, and you know your trading rules inside out. More importantly, you know that the only way to gain wealth is through flawless execution and discipline.

Here, *you apply what you know without thinking about it*. This is the ultimate goal of all traders – to become an emotionless and mechanical trader.

10.2 Technical Mastery – The Journey

Now that you've gotten a better view of how pullbacks can work in your favour, I believe it is wise to think about ways you can incorporate them into your own trading routine. More importantly, you need to consider how you can leverage on this knowledge.

If you want to integrate market pullbacks into your existing trading system, start off with a few rules and test your new system through back testing, forward testing or both. If you decide to have market pullbacks as a stand alone trading system, then create some rules based on your own personality and proceed to test it as well. Which ever way you do it is fine, but the only way to figure out which is the better option is through *sheer amount of practice* and some logical thinking.

Since pullbacks work on any timeframes, be sure to pick the timeframe that suits you, your schedule and the frequency you want to trade. Remember that you can get many more setups on a 5 minute chart compared to a daily chart.

Make sure that you thoroughly understand *how* market pullbacks work, *when* they work and, more importantly, when they *don't* work. It's like learning to drive a car. No matter how good you think you are in driving, it won't be safe to drive unless you've taken a minimum amount of practice on the road in a secure environment (i.e. with an instructor). In the case of trading, that would involve trading on a demo account, test environment or just a small account.

Once you start applying technical analysis and technical pullbacks just like the way you have a conversation while driving, and you are completely congruent with your decision, you know you are already in the journey towards technical mastery.

10.3 Mind Mastery – Trading in The Zone

A trader (and now a friend) once told me that taking a trade is like David Beckham taking a penalty (kick) in the Champions League Finals or like Tiger Woods teeing off in the U.S. PGA. When David gets into the penalty box or each time Tiger drives the ball from the tee, they adjust and pre-frame the mindset that they want. They rehearse in their mind their plan of attack and they see, hear and feel what they are about to do before they do it.

This is where David or Tiger goes into the zone – a place where they are in their winning mindset. While they don't know what happens after they attack the ball, it doesn't matter, and it's not important because all they really want to do is to focus on *Now*.

Some people call this Trading in the Zone while others just acknowledge that you need to have the right state-of-mind to trade. Whatever you may call it, you need to learn how to find and be able to draw out the state-of-mind where you are most confident, most rational and most relax. More importantly, you need to be able to bring out that state-of-mind each time you trade the market.

This is imperative to help traders focus on what is important because decisions that they make when they trade the market should be logical and unbiased.

In a gist, this is mind mastery, and, believe it or not, it is the ***most valuable tool*** in your trading career. Hence, make sure to practice and work on it on a daily basis until you master it.

11 Further Development

Thank you for purchasing this book.

The fact that you are reading this section now, it means that you probably want to develop your trading skills further.

Market Pullback

> If you want to explore the idea of trading market pullbacks seriously, or if you want to incorporate it into your own trading routine, I would like to invite you to visit www.MarketApprentice.com, where you can learn the step by step approach of trading the pullbacks.
>
> I have spent a good 8 months writing this book and I've come to the conclusion that learning to trade can be made more efficient through the use of other mediums. Learning should be interactive and that can be done with the advancement of technology. Hence, I've created Market Apprentice half way writing this book.
>
> Market Apprentice is an online trading academy designed to help **serious traders** approach the market with support and guidance. If you are serious about trading, then make sure to check out the academy because you might become an Apprentice trader sooner or later.

Mind Mastery

> Besides that, you can also consider taking your trading psychology to the next level through a comprehensive self-coaching program which I wrote. This is the 30 Day Trading Transformation and you can get your copy here today - www.30DayTradingTransformation.com
>
> Traders can learn to trade using the conscious and unconscious mind, thus, allowing traders to manage your own emotions, discipline and self control at a much more

professional level. I have developed these courses after receiving intensive training in the areas of Neuro Linguistic Programming (NLP) and Hypnosis.

If you do like this book and want others to enjoy what you did, do consider leaving a **positive review** on Amazon.com. This is also important because I have had some negative reviews from unverified buyers who are deliberately trying to discredits other reviews. While I continue to find ways to remove them, I ask for your review to counter them too.

You can do so even if you did not purchase the book from Amazon by posting or even liking the book here. Because Amazon is so competitive, your positive rating counts even if you decide to keep it short.

Lastly, thank you very much for your time. I wish you nothing but success, and I hope to see you soon at www.MarketApprentice.com.

Regards,

Alwin Ng

Trader & Coach
info@MarketApprentice.com

www.MarketApprentice.com

This Page is Blank

This Page is Blank